The Provoked Wife

THE NEW MERMAIDS

General Editor: Brian Gibbons
Professor of English Literature, University of Münster

THE NEW MERMAIDS

J.Miller. Sc.

The Provoked Wife

JOHN VANBRUGH

Edited by
JAMES L. SMITH

LONDON/A & C BLACK

NEW YORK/W W NORTON

Reissued 1993
Reprinted 1995
by A & C Black (Publishers) Limited
35 Bedford Row, London WC1R 4JH
ISBN 0–7136–3794–3

First published in this form 1974
by Ernest Benn Limited

Published in the United States of America by
W. W. Norton and Company Inc.
500 Fifth Avenue, New York, N.Y. 10110
ISBN 0–393–90067–3

A CIP catalogue record for this book
is available from the British Library.

Printed and bound in Great Britain by
Biddles Ltd, Guildford and King's Lynn

CONTENTS

TO

J. S. G.

G. R. Y.

ACKNOWLEDGEMENTS

MY CHIEF DEBT is to the handsome edition of Vanbrugh's *Works* prepared by Bonamy Dobrée and Geoffrey Webb (1927–28). I have also made use of the collected editions of Leigh Hunt (1840), W. C. Ward (1893), and A. E. H. Swain (1896), of the separate edition of *The Provoked Wife* in *The Chief British Dramatists*, ed. Brander Matthews and Paul Robert Lieder (n.d.), and of Thaler's edition in *Representative English Comedies, IV: Dryden and his Contemporaries*, ed. Charles Mills Gayley and Alwin Thaler (New York, 1936). Curt A. Zimansky's valuable edition for the Regents Restoration Drama Series (1969) has saved me from many blunders. My introduction and commentary have profited from these works, and from Laurence Whistler's biographical study, the several critical essays of Bernard Harris, and the theatrical and textual studies of Antony Coleman and Frank M. Patterson. Details of these and other helpful studies may be found on pp. xxxi–ii.

Many colleagues have patiently answered my enquiries, but I owe a special debt to Mr F. C. Mather and Dr K. M. Hall. The glosses translating French passages in the play were kindly supplied by Dr J. W. Scott. I am also grateful to Miss J. A. C. Morshead and Mr K. E. Jones of Southampton University Library, and to Miss Margaret Woodward, of Willow Grove, Chislehurst, who explained to me Heartfree's 'under scanty quilted petticoat'. No acknowledgement can express my gratitude to the unfailing kindness of Miss Serena Brown.

J.L.S.

'So, how d'ye like my shapes now?'
Garrick as Sir John Brute in the revised scenes

INTRODUCTION

THE AUTHOR

I'm in with captain Vanburgh at the present,
A most sweet-natur'd gentleman, and pleasant;
He writes your comedies, draws schemes, and models,
And builds dukes' houses upon very odd hills.
    ('Tonson' to 'Congreve' in Rowe's 'The Reconcilement')

SIR JOHN VANBRUGH, soldier, dramatist, architect, theatre manager, herald, and sometime Comptroller of the Royal Works, was born in London in January 1664, the ninth of nineteen children and the eldest surviving son. His father was a sugar-baker of Flemish descent, his mother the daughter of Sir Dudley Carleton. By 1667 the family had moved to Chester, but it is not known if John was educated there. He was commissioned ensign in the Earl of Huntingdon's Regiment on 30 January 1686 and resigned in August the same year, when the troops were ordered to the Channel Islands. Arrested in France in the autumn of 1688, he was imprisoned at Calais in 1690, transferred to Vincennes at his own cost in 1691, and to the Bastille on Louis XIV's orders in 1692. By the end of November he was back in England, released on parole in an exchange of prisoners. After duty as an auditor for the Southern division of Lancaster, he was commissioned captain in Lord Berkeley's Regiment in 1696, served until it was disbanded two years later, and took up the rank again in a new regiment raised by the earl of Huntingdon in 1702.

By this time Vanbrugh had commenced dramatist. November 1696 saw *The Relapse* at Drury Lane, followed by *I Aesop* in December and *II Aesop* the next March. In April 1697 *The Provoked Wife* was staged at the rival theatre in Lincoln's Inn Fields. Half a dozen adaptations followed. Dancourt's *La Maison de Campagne* appeared at Drury Lane in 1698 as *The Country House*. In 1700 came a version of Fletcher's *The Pilgrim*, for which Dryden wrote his matchless *Secular Masque*, and in 1702 *The False Friend*, from *Le Traître Puni*, which Le Sage had already taken from a Spanish comedy by Rojas Zorrilla. For Betterton's company at Lincoln's Inn Fields, Vanbrugh joined with Walsh and Congreve in adapting Molière's *Monsieur de Pourceaugnac* as *Squire Trelooby*, performed in 1704. When the actors moved to their new house in the Haymarket the next year, Vanbrugh obliged them with *The Confederacy*, a brilliant adaptation of Dancourt's *Les Bourgeoises à la Mode*, and a version of Molière's *Le Dépit Amoureux* which was rightly titled *The Mistake*. *The Cuckold in Conceit*, from Molière's *Le Cocu Imaginaire*, was acted in 1707 but is not known to have been printed.

Meanwhile Vanbrugh had embarked on several more careers. As a wit, a Whig, and a clubbable man, he was trebly welcome to Jacob Tonson's influential Kit Cat club. Charles Montagu, later earl of Halifax, helped his theatrical career; other members hired him as an architect. He built Castle Howard for the earl of Carlisle, Claremont for the duke of Newcastle, Kimbolton for the duke of Manchester, and Stowe for Viscount Cobham. Betterton's new theatre in the Haymarket was designed by Vanbrugh, built with Kit Cat money, and managed unsuccessfully by Vanbrugh and another Kit Cat, William Congreve. Blenheim Palace was the grandest of Vanbrugh's country houses, a fitting tribute to a national hero paid by one Kit Cat to another. Building began in 1705, and when Vanbrugh resigned from the Surveyorship in 1716—after ten years of delay, feud, financial crisis, political squabble, and the duchess of Marlborough—the house was still unfinished and his costs unpaid. Vanbrugh's other crown employments were less arduous. Through Carlisle's influence, he had been appointed Comptroller of the Royal Works in 1702, Carlisle Herald Extraordinary in 1703, and Clarenceux King of Arms in 1704. In this last capacity he went to Hanover in 1706 to invest George with the Garter, and when George arrived in England in 1714, Vanbrugh was the first man that he knighted.

Vanbrugh married Henrietta Yarborough at York in 1719, when he was fifty-five and she was twenty-six. It was a happy match, but not a long one. Choked by an inflammation of the throat, Vanbrugh died in London on 26 March 1726, and was buried in the family vault beneath the north aisle of Wren's church of St Stephen Walbrook. He left a widow who survived him fifty years, a son who died in 1745 of wounds sustained at the battle of Fontenoy, and an unfinished comedy, *A Journey to London*, which Colley Cibber completed as *The Provoked Husband*. It was staged in 1728.

THE PLAY

How Van wants grace, who never wanted wit!

(Pope, Ep. II. i)

Although *The Provoked Wife* was not performed until after the success of *The Relapse*, there is evidence to suggest it had been drafted some years earlier. Cibber thought so, and in 1698 Vanbrugh shrugged the play aside as something 'writ many years ago, and when

I was very young'; it may even be the comedy which Voltaire says he wrote while imprisoned in the Bastille in 1692.[1] Like most early plays, it owes a handsome debt to other dramatists. The leisurely unfolding of the simple plot recalls the spacious movement of *The Man of Mode*, and both find room for long debates comparing the morality of the sexes. A discussion on feminine modesty at the playhouse echoes something from the second act of Wycherley's *Plain Dealer*. Madamoiselle and Rasor are the soubrette and clever lackey made popular by Molière, and Lady Fancyfull owes part of her affectation to the Frenchified Melantha in Dryden's *Marriage à la Mode*. Even the disposition of the major characters finds a parallel in Otway's farce *The Soldier's Fortune*, where a provoked wife again is poised between her husband and her gallant, while her niece moves into matrimony with the gallant's friend.

Vanbrugh's central theme of marital disharmony was not a new one in the comedy of manners. Etherege and Wycherley and Dryden had employed it, so had Shadwell in both *Epsom Wells* and *Bury Fair*. But in these plays the crucial action still concerns a pair or two of witty lovers; the disaffected married couples merely form a sub-plot interest. When they seek to gain admittance to the emancipated circle, and even try to poach upon their privileged preserves, they are rejected by the younger set with scornful laughter which the dramatist endorses. Wycherley demands no sympathy for Pinchwife in *The Country Wife*, nor Otway in *The Soldier's Fortune* for Sir Davy Dunce. In the comedy of manners, old buffers who marry young wives out of lust deserve none. Nor do Margery and Lady Fidget in *The Country Wife* or Lady Cockwood in *She Would if She Could* or Lady Touchwood in *The Double Dealer*. Adulterous wives may be rustic ingenues, affected hypocrites, or withered flirts. Always they are grasping sensualists devoid of moral scruple and eager to deceive a husband, chase a rake, or blackmail a handsome nephew into bed. They are presented with detachment, and satirized for their hypocrisy or jealousy or insatiate—and often thwarted —lust.

Vanbrugh's play adopts a different strategy, which links it rather with a group of marriage comedies begun by Southerne in *The Wives' Excuse* in 1691 and terminated in 1707 with Farquhar's *The Beaux' Stratagem*.[2] Their main plots all derive from marital imprisonment, with a pair of witty lovers to round out supporting scenes. When the

[1] See Colley Cibber, *An Apology for the Life of Mr Colley Cibber*, ed. R. W. Lowe (1889), I, 216; Vanbrugh, *A Short Vindication of The Relapse and The Provok'd Wife from Immorality and Prophaneness* (1698), p. 49; Voltaire, *Lettres Philosophiques*, ed. F. A. Taylor, 2nd edn. (Oxford, 1946), p. 75.
[2] See A. H. Scouten, 'Notes toward a history of Restoration comedy', *PQ*, XLV (1966), 62–70.

disaffected partners move towards adultery, they violate a moral code which they approve. The dramatists do not dismiss them with contempt. Their infidelities are shown with understanding and a measure of excuse. A serious consideration of this theme of marital disharmony is common to all three of Vanbrugh's major plays. He broached it in the Amanda-Loveless plot of *The Relapse* and in the Loverule sub-plot of *A Journey to London*. In *The Provoked Wife* it is his chief concern.

The foolish marriage of Sir John and Lady Brute provides the main plot of the play. Both have acted selfishly and are frank enough to say so. She married him for his estate; he married her because she would not sleep with him on other terms. The result is a miserable stalemate which drives him to debauchery and her to thoughts of infidelity. In his other marriage comedies Vanbrugh takes the easy course of siding with one spouse against the other. Both partners here are shown to be at fault, and Vanbrugh takes them through the consequences of their folly with a clear-sighted tolerance which nicely balances our sympathy and censure.

Sir John is so devoted to the glorious manly pleasures of being very drunk and very slovenly that he has generally been given over as a brute beyond redemption. A provoked wife necessitates a provoking husband. Yet Sir John does not deserve our total condemnation. At home he may well be unbearable; abroad he can be fun. Like Wildfire and Sir William Rant in Shadwell's city comedy *The Scowrers*, Sir John aspires to be 'a man of quality'. He regrets he ever kept the company of sneaking fools 'that went to church, said grace to their meat, and had not the least tincture of quality about 'em' (II.i.262–4). He leaves his visitors abruptly to confer about the serious business of a nightly frolic, and his greatest boast is that he is 'hand and glove' with my Lord Rake. Tom Brown's letter from 'Melanissa to Alexis' indicates his usual activities, and might well stand for an eye-witness's comment on Sir John's adventures in the play. The setting, appropriately, is 'The Rose' or 'The Blue Posts' and

> ten to one but a merry frolic is proposed; the quarters of some ill-natured coquette are to be beaten up, and her poor windows must feel the sad effects of their heroic valour. But while they are carrying on this attack with unparalleled vigour and gallantry, behold the superintendent of the night, with his trusty and well-beloved janizaries, takes these sparks together by the ears, with their perukes, hats, and muffs lying by them. The embroidered coat is all over covered with dirt and blood, the well-adjusted cravat torn to rags, the sword either broken or carried off in the tumult; and thus, after a well-favoured drubbing, our sparks make a shift to crawl home to their lodgings, if the nocturnal magistrate and his cannibals don't

hurry them to New-Prison, or the Round-House, the usual sanctuary of such adventurers.[3]

The frolics of Sir John are common form among the bullies of his day, and no doubt Vanbrugh aims a swingeing mock-heroic satire at the dissipated social code they represent. The trouble is that in the theatre these scenes of crude debauchery create an atmosphere of exhilarating, riotous misrule. And when Vanbrugh substituted for Sir John's disguise as Parson Hiccup one in which he dresses up as Lady Brute, the scenes became still funnier. No reviewer omits a tribute to their redeeming 'waggishness', 'boisterous comedy', 'delicious impudence', or 'extraordinarily good fooling', and *The Times* even rises to commend their 'certain Rabelaisian exuberance of crapulousness'.[4] This mood continues when Sir John arrives back home, all dirt and bloody and drunk as a lord, insisting he must kiss his wife and tumble her and taste a cup of her cold tea before they go to bed together. In real life no doubt his conduct is indefensible, but within the comic confines of the play it receives our joyous approbation. These scenes contain some of Vanbrugh's most distinctive work, and celebrate his pleasure in life-enhancing energy, farcical high spirits, and all the anarchic, filthy, joyous bestiality of man. Sir John is Vanbrugh's Falstaff, and his vices our delight.

Lady Brute, by contrast, is mistress of all the virtues proper to a woman of her station; she has youth and beauty, charm and wit, intelligence, maturity, and a moral sense. All are apparent in the opening scene. Congreve first shows us Millamant in St James's Park, scattering epigrams among a flock of beaux. Vanbrugh opens with the Brutes at home and lets us overhear their daily jangle. She honestly confesses the ignoble motives which impelled her to the match, and in an intimate duologue with her niece Bellinda admits her heart is wandering. But Lady Brute is not of the Touchwood tribe. To begin with, she is not naturally lewd, but only driven by her husband's cruelty to look elsewhere for kindness. Such a wife will seldom ramble, till a husband shows her the way. And since Sir John is a disgusting bully, braggart, brawler, rake-hell, coward, misogamist, whoremonger, snob, and sot, who wears dirty linen, smokes tobacco in the dining room, reels home drunk every night, and thinks to keep his wife honest by continual persecution, it may be thought she has excuse enough to cuckold him, and even our

[3] Tom Brown, *Amusements serious and comical and Other Works*, ed. A. L. Hayward (1927), pp. 130–1.
[4] *Theatre World*, XLVI (May 1950), 8; the *Evening Standard*, 24 March 1950; *The Times*, 6 October 1936; the *Daily Telegraph*, 6 October 1936; *The Times*, 15 January 1919.

approval if she does. Secondly, at some cost to the credibility of his character the man who tempts her is not another Dorimant or Horner, who wakes up with one mistress thinking of the next and planning the subjection of a third. Constant is his name and constancy his nature; for two years he has wooed her with unremitting fervour, sustained without a single favour only by his hopes. For Lady Brute is no coquette. Even when she toys with immorality, she still preserves a rigid moral sense, and will not pretend to encourage a gallant before she is resolved to gratify him. Lastly, this decisive moral sense is so entrenched it will not leave her. She may be savagely provoked and sweetly tempted, but still the final choice, the ultimate responsibility for cuckoldom, is hers. Adultery for Lady Brute is not a casual pleasure but a yielding to temptation, a deliberate violation of the moral code by which she lives. She would if she could, but she cannot even bring herself to speak the word. She tries to argue herself into adultery, but her intelligent attempts to read the marriage contract as if it were not made before God are as unpersuasive as Constant's sophistries, which puzzle but don't convince. Would that they did. Torn between conscience and inclination, she can neither encourage Constant nor reject him, neither yield nor deny. She is as far from Madamoiselle's 'je m'abandonne à toi!' as she is from the austere purity of Mrs Friendall in *The Wives' Excuse*, who repulses her lover with:

> Every Woman carries her Cross in this World: A Husband happens to be mine, and I must bear it, as well as I can.   (V.iii)

For Lady Brute, who cannot play the harlot or the martyr, it is an impossible dilemma.

It gives Vanbrugh a few problems too. For how can this sympathetic woman be the heroine of a realistic comedy? She seems closer to *A Doll's House* than to *The Country Wife*. She is no Margery or Fidget. Satire wilts before the firmness of her conscience and the integrity of her mind. Where, then, lies the comedy? Partly in the wit. For Lady Brute is too wise to take herself too seriously, and by a delicate self-mockery succeeds in distancing herself from her dilemma and the audience from her. And when she dares to stand upon her virtue, someone is sure to undercut the lofty tone. This is the dynamic of her altercation with Bellinda in the opening scene, and it animates such brief exchanges as

LADY BRUTE
   'Tis a hard fate I should not be believed.
SIR JOHN
   'Tis a damned atheistical age, wife.   (V.ii.33–4)

Vanbrugh distances us from her in other ways. Sometimes she acts

in comic ignorance of facts the audience already knows, as when she
settles down to cards with Constant unaware that Lady Fancyfull is
scouring all the taverns of the town to find Sir John and send him
home post-haste to spoil their sport. Sometimes Vanbrugh flings
her into compromising situations, where her innocence is made to
seem lascivious and her consequent embarrassment a mask for lewd
intent. (Here Lady Brute is like the lovable heroine of every situation-
comedy series on television.[5]) Thus when Sir John insists on breaking
down her closet door to get at her cold tea, he finds—of course—poor
Constant hiding there; and when he drives her from the room in
fury, she discovers she has run for shelter straight into Constant's
open arms. These devices are most sharply focussed upon Lady
Brute's seduction in Spring Garden. Constant opens with his usual
chop-logic, then rises to romantic ardours in blank verse which
Vanbrugh wrote as prose. The change of gear alerts us to the pressure
of emotion in the scene, while hinting that the attitudes involved
are strained or false. When Lady Brute sustains the verse in her
replies, Constant grows bolder and his pentameters more wild (as
this relineation shows):

> Forgive me, therefore, since my hunger rages,
> If I at last grow wild and in my frenzy
> Force at least this from you.   (*Kissing her hand*)
> Or if you'd have my flame soar higher still,
> Then grant me this, and this, and this, and thousands more.
>   (*Kissing first her hand, then her neck.—Aside*)
> For now's the time; she melts into compassion.   (IV.iv.193–9)

His eloquent romantic posturing collapses into a rakish, cynical
aside. Blank verse becomes colloquial prose; the rhetoric was no
more than a cheap seducer's calculated trick. Though we are un-
deceived, however, Lady Brute remains comically unaware of
Constant's falsity. Confessing in a parallel aside how much her
coward virtue shuns the battle, she then confronts her lover with a
pose of outraged purity as false as his.

> O heavens! let me go

she protests, and Constant takes this for an invitation to go—with
her—into a private arbour. The hilarious physical combat which
ensues, he pulling her and she resisting, ends with Lady Brute's
half-serious, half-yielding cry of

> Ah, I'm lost!

Whereupon she is immediately saved. For Lady Fancyfull and

[5] I am indebted here to D. A. Nelson's unpublished thesis 'The laughing
comedy of the eighteenth century' (Ithaca, 1965), 61–76, a most valuable
account of the play.

Madamoiselle come rushing from the arbour to the utter confusion of the lovers, and the laughter of the audience, who knew that they were there in hiding all the time. This sustained juxtapositioning of contrasted attitudes and punctured tones, reinforced by gaps of awareness between audience and character, and by physical effects which border upon farce, keeps our sympathy detached from Lady Brute. Instead of pitying the moral problems of a provoked wife, we laugh at her ridiculous distress. The element of farce in Vanbrugh's play thus conditions our responses to the Brutes in different ways: it makes Sir John an amiable beast, and exposes to our laughter his more sympathetic wife.

Vanbrugh does not press these characters to any firm conclusion. He lets Lady Brute preserve her virtue by an accident, and when Sir John discovers Constant hiding in her closet, Vanbrugh saves him from a challenge by making him too drunk to stay awake. Next morning he puts his horns into his pocket and apologises to his wife's seducer. When the play ends, Lady Brute has been scared out of her wits, and her husband shaken in his faith that persecution will preserve his sexual monopoly. There may be some slight growth in self-awareness here, but the basic problem of their marital incompatibility has not been solved. Their situation when the curtain falls is exactly what it had been when it rose. The final scene does not transform Sir John into a golden-hearted good old man whose offer of a handsome maintenance shames Lady Brute into a deep-felt declaration of undying love. Such tender reconciliations are reserved for Sheridan's *The School for Scandal*. Nor is Constant so bedazzled by his mistress's virtue he gives over the pursuit and rests her mute, adoring worshipper, like Worthy at the end of *The Relapse*.

The English law permitted some less sentimental answers to the problem of an unsuccessful marriage, but none that Vanbrugh could adopt to give his play an honestly happy ending. The pair might separate by mutual consent, like Farquhar's Squire and Mrs Sullen and the Friendalls in *The Wives' Excuse*. No judicial process was required; marital relations might be taken up any time, and neither party could remarry. Alternatively, if one spouse refused to part, the other could sue in an ecclesiastical court for separation 'from bed and board'. Adultery was the one effective charge, to be proved upon one party only, and by independent witnesses free from all suspicion of collusion. The procedure was lengthy, expensive, and humiliating. Neither partner could remarry, and the husband—even when the injured party—was required to provide a separate maintenance. When Sir John considers this solution, Heartfree reminds him of the scandal and the cost:

SIR JOHN
   If I could but catch her adulterating, I might be divorced from
her by law.
HEARTFREE
   And so pay her a yearly pension, to be a distinguished cuckold.
(III.i.103–6)

In any case, separation is no answer for the Brutes. Sir John is too
afraid of Lady Brute's relations to thrust her out of doors, and too
wary of his honour to start an action. Neither could bring evidence
against the other. And a separation would not allow Lady Brute to
forget her conscience and dance off into adultery like Mrs Sullen.
This bleak outlook was to improve a little with the establishment of
parliamentary divorce in 1698. The injured party first obtained a
separation in an ecclesiastical court, then fought a successful action
for damages against the adulterer at law, and finally passed up
through Parliament a private bill dissolving the existing marriage
and freeing the petitioner to try again. Bellinda's reference to the
House of Lords may hint at this procedure, but in fact no English
woman was granted a divorce by Parliament before 1801.[6]

If Vanbrugh offers no solutions to the problem of a miserable
marriage, it is because in 1697 no solutions are available. And he will
not contrive the fraudulent or sentimental 'happy endings' found in
Farquhar or in Sheridan. This honesty does not reduce the play into
a simple piece of propaganda attacking the inadequate divorce laws
of the day. Vanbrugh concentrates upon the human frailties of Sir
John and Lady Brute, but even here he makes no final judgement.
They brought their marital unhappiness upon themselves, and he
is content to let them make the best of it they can.

Vanbrugh does not condemn all marriages because the Brutes
have failed. There is more hope for Heartfree and Bellinda, whose
wise and witty courtship forms the sub-plot of the play. The
economic pressures of the main plot are still present, though re-
versed. Bellinda is an independent fortune of ten thousand pound.
Like Lady Brute, she toys with marrying 'some odious man of
quality' to gain a coronet upon her coach, but the spectacle of Sir
John dead drunk in his great chair effectively deters her. What
though Heartfree is a younger brother, with nothing to depend on
but his debts?

   I can't say I would live with him in a cell upon love and bread and
   butter; but I had rather have the man I love, and a middle state
   of life, than that gentleman in the chair there, and twice your
   ladyship's splendour.   (V.ii.122–5)

[6] See G. S. Alleman, *Matrimonial Law and the Materials of Restoration
Comedy* (Philadelphia, 1942), pp. 106–41.

Heartfree approaches marriage with the same idealism tempered by the same shrewd commonsense. It is tempting to suppose him Vanbrugh's moral spokesman, the *honnête homme* whose sanity provides a norm against which the attitudes of others are arraigned. He embodies a conception of 'the man of quality' which is the antithesis of Sir John's. Lady Fancyfull is a female Foppington who believes her beauty has enslaved the world; Heartfree calls her to a reckoning, proscribes her affectation, and tells the audience what to think. With the same precision he lays bare the paradox of Constant's posture as a sentimental rake, who 'adores his mistress for being virtuous, and yet is very angry with her because she won't be lewd' (II.i.140–2). But here his role as *raisonneur* comes to an end. Heartfree finds lovers foolish because his view of woman is reductive. Her social graces do not charm him when he imagines her stripped to her stays, and when he contemplates her mind he finds there only viciousness and folly. His indifference is therefore based upon a partial fallacy. The social graces of a Lady Fancyfull might not survive his rigorous enquiry, but Vanbrugh has already shown us women endowed with honesty, intelligence, and wit. Heartfree encounters Bellinda in Act III, and in Act IV denies his name.

The marriage towards which this couple move, though not ideal, is clearly better than the selfish sexual alternatives around them. The Brutes' contract was a bargain driven by two selfish takers: he took possession of her body and she of his estate. Two years later, both regret the deal. Constant and Lady Fancyfull, the marriage-breakers of the play, are also selfish takers. Lady Brute sees Constant as a knight errant, but he rescues ladies from distress only to reserve them to himself. He speaks the common language of the Restoration rake—though it is not restricted to him only—and sees the sexual prize as food to be tasted, game to be hunted, or a town to be stormed. Even the seduction is pursued in egocentric terms: my sufferings, my flame, my hunger, and my frenzy. The selfish taking shown by Lady Fancyfull is much more vicious, for like her maid she is a coquette who uses sex to subjugate a man she never means to satisfy. When promises and kisses have set Rasor all afire, Madamoiselle dismisses him to cool off in the river. Her lady dreams of ruling over subjects who are all in love with her. When Heartfree will not be enslaved, she thinks he should be caned, locked in her closet, or satirized into subjection—though 'every lash I give him, perhaps, he'll take for a favour' (II.ii.120–1). These sadistic fantasies hint at a selfish, desperate frustration; they are Vanbrugh's Cave of Spleen.

Heartfree and Bellinda, by contrast, are honest givers willing to make sacrifices for their love: she to resign her social aspiration and he his rakish independence. Yet this is no clear marriage of true minds. Both see it as a gamble or a risk, an uncertain leap into the dark. Bellinda cannot know if Heartfree will ill-use her, and Heartfree is uncertain of himself. In the usual comedy of manners a rake who marries is at once transformed from the most fickle lover to the most constant husband in the world—a convention Vanbrugh ridiculed in Loveless's relapse. Heartfree was a rake who thought all women vicious; now he is as cynically contemptuous of men. He does not fear Bellinda will betray him, but that he will lack constancy himself and so encourage her to ramble the more he 'grows Sir John'. 'Marriage', says Constant, is 'a lottery in which there are a wondrous many blanks, yet there is one inestimable lot in which the only heaven on earth is written'. This from a man who spends his time attempting to seduce a miserable wife! It is a sentimental rapture (and in blank verse too) which the speaker does not base upon mature awareness of the world around him. Heartfree can agree with the ideal, 'for to be capable of loving one, doubtless is better than to possess a thousand. But', he adds (and drops back into prose), 'how far that capacity's in me, alas, I know not' (V.iv. 67–70,73–5). He sees, as Constant cannot, that human nature is frail and easily corruptible. And he knows he is no stronger than the rest.

Vanbrugh endorses Heartfree's doubts in the sceptical finale. He puts the faith of both the lovers to the test and finds it wanting. They believe at once the unsupported accusations of a disguised woman and an unsigned letter, and the match is broken off with bitter words. When an implausible denouement reunites them, Constant sings a warning song about the sexual maladjustment of a newly married couple. And as they leave for church, Heartfree will commit himself for one night's lodging only, while Bellinda casts a cautionary glance at the fate of surly husbands like Sir John. These are no more than witty jokes, of course. But it is not a wholly optimistic final curtain.

In the two triangles of his plot and sub-plot, Vanbrugh articulates six contrasting attitudes to love and marriage. In many ways the play is like a Shavian debate. In *Misalliance*, for example, nothing happens beyond a wealth of talk, and when this needs replenishment, an aeroplane crashes into the greenhouse and out steps a lady acrobat named Lina Szczepanowska; later in the same first act an unknown man with a revolver takes refuge in a portable Turkish bath. *The Provoked Wife* employs the same technique; there is the same bare minimum of plot and maximum of clever conversation, the same short-winded farcical contrivance to keep the play from flagging.

Vanbrugh himself confessed his play contained 'no mighty Plot' inexorably unwinding from the first scene to the last. The Brutes end where they began, the Heartfrees have a short sprint to the church. Two attempts are made to link the different actions. Like Foppington again, Lady Fancyfull has a hand in both. Her interest in Heartfree makes Bellinda make her jealous, and her revenge strives to expose Constant's affair with Lady Brute. Secondly, this crisis in the Brutes' relationship precipitates the marriage of the Heartfrees, just as Hero's slander brings together Benedick and Beatrice in *Much Ado*. Both plots avoid the complications which perplex the comedies of Wycherley and Congreve. Vanbrugh prefers the simple situation which allows more play to character and debate. The chief end of his intrigues is to bring people on the stage; he attacked

> the crowding a Comedy with a great deal of Intricate Plot. I believe I cou'd shew, that the chief entertainment, as well as the Moral, lies much more in the Characters and the Dialogue, than in the Business and the Event.[7]

Vanbrugh's dialogue justifies this confidence. He has a perfect ear for Heartfree's vigorous and virile tone with Constant, his intricate debates with Lady Brute, her composure with the cantankerous Sir John and air-born impudence with Bellinda. The lovers are less polished and more natural than Millamant and Mirabell; they also have much less to say to one another. Congreve builds his play on scenes of witty courtship, but Vanbrugh concentrates on intimate exchanges between two persons of one sex. His conversations therefore lack the element of sexual competition and display which drives a Congreve dialogue along. His speakers are not talking to impress each other but to amuse themselves. They do not need to cap each epigram; the wit is leisurely, the tone relaxed. As Walpole and Cibber realized, this is the secret of Vanbrugh's lounging style:

> We are entertained, not surprised or struck. We are in good company while with him; and have neither adventures nor bons mots to repeat afterwards. It is the proof of consummate art in a comic writer, when you seem to have passed your time at the theatre as you might have done out of it—it proves he has exactly hit the style, manners, and character of his cotemporaries.

> And indeed his Wit and Humour was so little laboured, that his most entertaining Scenes seem'd to be no more than his common Conversation committed to Paper.[8]

The common conversation of this play has many voices. A single duologue between Lady Brute and Bellinda rises from grave to gay,

---

[7] *Short Vindication*, p. 57.
[8] Horace Walpole, 'Thoughts on Comedy', *Works* (1798), II, 316; Cibber, *An Apology*, I, 219.

climbs to a peak of comic mockery, then takes a sudden plunge into thoughtfulness or frankness. Constant rides a more spectacular switchback from the heights of sentimentalism down to honest slang. Lord Rake talks in military metaphors, Lady Fancyfull in lards and raptures, Madamoiselle in broken English, and Rasor delights in legal mumbo-jumbo. Even Jo the porter has his voice: 'whip! they were gone', he says, 'like a maidenhead at fifteen' (IV.ii.113–4). There are canting terms, parodic platitudes, sequences of 'character' writing, bully-beaux' slang, a welter of French, songs, asides, soliloquies, blank verse, rhyming tags, couplets, puns, paradoxes—and even pantomime.

This last is inevitable, for the exuberant vitality of Vanbrugh's comic style moves speedily from words into events. As Hazlitt saw, his *doubles-entendres* are equivocal situations, and his best jokes all practical devices. Like Shaw, he is a natural comedian. His scenes of action throw together people who at all costs should be kept apart. Sir John and Lady Fancyfull always appear to interrupt the lovers at the most inopportunely right wrong moment. He piles up incident on incident with dizzying hilarity, as in the mock-seduction scene of Rasor and Madamoiselle. And he is a master of mounting embarrassment. Contemptuous of two women whom they take for common prostitutes, Constant and Heartfree are eager to resign them to Sir John; whereupon the distressed ladies are forced to unmask and Constant thrown into still more confusion to prevent Sir John from picking up his wife as a cheap whore. The accelerated pacing of these scenes, where characters leap from one crisis into another still more dangerous, exonerates the play's denouement from the frequent charge of carelessness or haste. No doubt Lady Fancyfull's malicious letter and disguise are unpersuasive; so is Rasor's late entry, instantaneous intrigue and sudden resolution to confess all and be saved. But on the stage these problems disappear. When events are so funny and move so fast there is no time to think how they arose. It is not necessary to assume that Vanbrugh planned his comic structure in this way; he is a dramatist by instinct, and his instinct is generally right. Certainly, this element of farcical contrivance strengthens his theatrical appeal. Like Miss Szczepanowska's aeroplane, it saves the play from the aridity of an intellectual debate. And it keeps the sceptical last act from turning sour. Vanbrugh is a comic realist. He does not idealize human nature like a sentimentalist nor vilify its failings like a cynic. He sees the world for what it is and laughs at what he sees. His laughter is the measure of an ultimate affection for the men and women he creates. Through laughter Sir John is humanized, Lady Brute rendered more ridiculous than pitiful, the Heartfrees seen with modest hope, and even Lady Fancyfull excused. For five acts no one spares her a good word.

But when she is unmasked and humiliated at the end, Bellinda
understands her jealous passion and finds she can forgive her.

STAGE HISTORY

His 'Provoked Wife', is full of such indecent sentiments and
allusions, as ought to explode it out of all reputable society.
(Hugh Blair, *Lectures on Rhetoric and Belles Lettres*)

On 25 March 1695, Betterton, Mrs Bracegirdle, Mrs Barry, and
half a dozen more of the best actors rebelled against the tyranny of
Rich at Drury Lane and set up a rival company in a converted
tennis court in Lincoln's Inn Fields. They prospered. To fortify
the rump, Cibber turned author with *Love's Last Shift* and Captain
Vanbrugh was persuaded to dash off a sequel. The immediate success of *The Relapse* opened doors at both the theatres. According to
Cibber, Charles Montagu heard Vanbrugh read *The Provoked Wife*
'in its looser Sheets', and engaged him to revise it for the rebel
company. The play opened at Lincoln's Inn Fields in April 1697,
with a glittering cast led by Betterton himself—a thick-set, cor-
pulent man of grumbling voice—as Sir John. Lady Brute was played
by Elizabeth Barry, his favourite leading lady, with beautiful Anne
Bracegirdle as Bellinda and dashing Jack Verbruggen—who had just
created Loveless at Drury Lane—as Constant. In 1700 they were
the first Millamant and Mirabell. With such a cast and such a play
success was guaranteed, and Vanbrugh inevitably came under heavy
fire next year from Collier's *Short View of the Immorality and Profaneness of the English Stage*. Starting from the usual premise that
'The business of *Plays* is to recomend Virtue, and discountenance
Vice', Collier fell upon *The Provoked Wife* because Lord Rake sings
'a Drunken Atheistical Catch', Rasor falsifies Scripture, Sir John
dresses as a clergyman for his frolic, Lady Brute talks smut and
thinks adultery, and Constant is a rake who escapes scot-free with
the character of a fine gentleman. Vanbrugh had declared his
modest aims in an aggressive preface to *The Relapse*. With an
apology for offending 'any honest gentlemen of the town, whose
friendship or good word is worth the having', he admitted no other
design 'than to divert (if possible) some part of their spleen, in spite
of their wives and their taxes'. Replying to Collier in his *Short
Vindication*, Vanbrugh took a more didactic line:

For the Business of Comedy is to shew People what they shou'd
do, by representing them upon the Stage, doing what they shou'd
not. .. The Stage is a Glass for the World to view it self in;

People ought therefore to see themselves as they are; if it makes their Faces too Fair, they won't know they are Dirty, and by consequence will neglect to wash 'em.[9]

Grant this, and everything falls into place. Sir John's 'Business throughout the Play, is a visible Burlesque upon his Character'; Constant's vices are laid open as well as his virtues; when Lady Brute says virtue's an ass ' 'tis not Virtue she exposes, but her self'. And as for her proposed adultery, why,

since she was Regular while he was kind, the Fable may be a useful Admonition to Men who have Wives, and wou'd keep 'em to themselves, not to build their Security so entirely upon their Ladies Principles, as to venture to pull from under her all the Political Props of her Virtue. (p. 69)

There is more wit than wisdom in these arguments, and the firm moral structure of the play does not require their slender underpinning.

The debate continued with a flurry of pamphlets and some threats of legal action. Shorthand writers were stationed in the theatres as spies, and in 1701 Betterton's company was indicted before the King's Bench for speaking profanities in *The Provoked Wife* and other plays.[10] To judge from *Hell upon Earth; or the Language of the Playhouse* (*c.* 1706) the controversy had the most bracing effect upon the box-office, for

the horrid Comedies of *Love for Love*, *The Provok'd Wife*, and *The Spanish Fryar*, are frequently acted in all places to which the Players come. The more they have been expos'd by Mr. *Collier* and others, the more they seem to be admir'd![11]

On 19 January 1706, Vanbrugh revived the play with most of the original cast at the new theatre which he had built for Betterton's company in the Haymarket. It was played at Lincoln's Inn Fields on 21 December 1715, at Drury Lane on 11 January 1726, and at Covent Garden on 28 March 1733; in London and the provinces it remained in the stock repertory until near the end of the century. To bring the play within the bounds of 'genteel comedy', the character of Sir John Brute was softened as the century advanced. Quin inherited the role from Betterton *via* Keene, and faithfully preserved the grumbling coarseness of the character. So did Macklin, whose ill-mannered sot made no attempt at mellowness. But Colley Cibber, who played the part at Drury Lane, was a lightweight actor

[9] *Short Vindication*, pp. 45–6.
[10] See J. W. Krutch, *Comedy and Conscience after the Restoration* (New York, 1924), pp. 169–73.
[11] Quoted from W. C. Ward, ed., *Sir John Vanbrugh* (1893), I, xxxii.

with a piping voice whose great successes were in Shallow, Fondle-wife, and Foppington. According to *The Prompter* (19 November 1734), his Brute was *'beautifully ridiculous'* but in a foppish, gentle-manly style. Garrick's dissipated *roué*, with swagger cane and modish hat cocked at a jaunty angle, lent such authority to the reading that Ryder's efforts to restore the guts of Vanbrugh's character in 1786 met with a mixed reception.[12]

Meanwhile, judicious cuts were grooming Lady Brute into a sentimental heroine who bears Sir John's brutality with a martyr's smile. In Bell's edition, 'as performed at the Theatre-Royal, Covent-Garden' (1794), she does not debate her marriage vow and conclude that a gallant is worth forty on't. Instead, her opening soliloquy is sliced in half, and a new ending substituted:

> Perhaps a good part of what I suffer from my husband, may be a judgment upon me for my cruelty to my lover—But hold—let me go no further—I think I have a right to alarm this surly brute of mine—but if I know my heart—it will never let me go so far as to injure him.   (p. 10)

Thus is morality preserved and the comedy extinguished. The whole text is disinfected. Lady Brute makes no mention of the torrent of love or the sluice of desire, and her coward virtue is not allowed to say how much it shuns the battle. Constant never speaks of strait-laced chastity or the sordid slavery in marriage. 'Debauching' be-comes 'deluding' and Sir John is 'sacrificed' instead of 'crucified'. One fine interpolation escaped the censor's eye. When Rasor carries out his drunken master, the actor ends the scene with a filthy broken couplet:

> *My master's asleep, in his chair, and a snoring,*
> *My lady's abroad, and—Oh rare matrimony!*   (p. 93)

There is even a futile effort to redeem Sir John. After Bellinda's last line, he closes the play with:

> Surly I may be, stubborn I am not,
> For I have both forgiven and forgot;
> If so, be these our judges, Mrs. Pert,
> 'Tis more by my goodness, than your desert.   (p. 113)

Despite this grotesque emasculation, by 1800 the play was virtually 'exploded' from the stage. It did not reappear until 1919, when the Incorporated Stage Society mounted two matinees at the King's

[12] I am indebted here to K. A. Burnim, *David Garrick, Director* (Pittsburgh, 1961), pp. 176-7, and Antony Coleman, 'Sir John Brute on the eighteenth century stage', *Restoration and Eighteenth Century Theatre Research*, VIII (1969), 41-6.

Hall, London (12–14 January). Margaret Halstan was Lady Brute, Lewis Casson Constant, Baliol Holloway Heartfree, and Marie Rambert Madamoiselle. Hubert Carter played Sir John in the Quin tradition, with bald head, swollen stomach, false teeth, and fuddled wits. The *Sunday Times* admired the play's 'strange mixture of coarseness and courtliness' (19 January 1919); the *Referee* called it 'filth', and cited Collier with approval. In John Fernald's production for the Embassy Theatre, London (5 October 1936), Mervyn Johns reverted to the Garrick style, 'delicately clowning' through the crudities (*The Times*, 6 October). At the Arts Theatre Club (22 March 1950), Russell Waters brought back the right 'lickerish barbarism' to the role (the *Observer*, 26 March), but Max Adrian's direction swamped the play in irrelevant high jinks. Lady Brute sang an aria by Purcell, Lord Rake deafened the stalls with a song entitled 'We shall want time to be lewd in', and the evening ended with a musical epilogue and country dance. The Guildford Repertory Company staged a revival in March 1953. Ten years later, Eileen Atkins and Trevor Martin played the Brutes for the Prospect Theatre Company. The play opened in a caravan theatre on Binsey Green, Oxford, in June, transferred to the Georgian Theatre in Richmond, Yorkshire, and then to the Vaudeville on 24 July. John Warner and Dinsdale Landen strengthened the London cast, but it was not a successful run. Toby Robertson's production lacked West End glitter, and Trevor Martin's 'gruff villainy' reminded the *Evening Standard* of Barrie's Captain Hook (25 July). The dramatist David Hare directed a sprightly revival at the Palace Theatre, Watford (21 February 1973), with Prunella Scales and Trevor Peacock as the Brutes and Sheila Reid as Lady Fancyfull. Unconventional attractions included semi-abstract sets and lighting, music adapted from Ennio Morricone, and a discreet display of frontal nudity from Michael Graham Cox, who played Heartfree. At the Greenwich Theatre four months later (14 June), Fenella Fielding appeared as Lady Fancyfull in a fluffy blonde wig trimmed up with bright blue ribbons, and instantly stole the show. James Grout turned in a raucous fruity Brute, and Sheila Allen supported gently as his wife. But Frederick Proud's slapdash production presented Vanbrugh's moral comedy as a Feydeau farce; 'and as a farce', the *Daily Telegraph* reported (15 June), 'this tale of a wife's peccadillo simply fails to hold the stage'. Of recent years, there have been a number of amateur revivals, by New College, Oxford (31 October 1950), The Royal Academy of Dramatic Art (29 November 1961), Oxford University Dramatic Society (31 October 1966), The London Academy of Music and Dramatic Art (28 November 1969), and the Questors Theatre, Ealing (6 May 1972). Reviews of these twelve productions suggest some new perspectives. The central role is clearly Sir John Brute's. He affords the richest acting opportunities, and his drunken orgy always forms the climax of the show. Lady Brute is usually considered in relationship to him and not to Constant who, like Heartfree and Bellinda, is sometimes demoted to the small print at the foot of the review. By contrast, Lady Fancyfull takes on a new importance, together with the mock-seduction of Rasor and Madamoiselle. What comes across most strongly in performance are those characters who verge on caricature and those scenes where Vanbrugh celebrates drunkenness, debauchery, and the unbridled lechery of man. The hearty fun derived from these bestial appetites in action corrects the academic emphasis upon the play's more 'intellectual' debates. But it is in the union of these qualities that Vanbrugh's unique excellence resides. A director sensitive to the head and heart and guts of Vanbrugh's play may well restore it to that position in the modern theatre which for upwards of two centuries it has been denied.

In the twenty years since the above was written, the play has been given at least three London productions. Peter Wood's revival for the National Theatre was presented on 29 October 1980 within the proscenium arch of the Lyttelton Theatre; much of the action was set near or sometimes on the frozen River Thames, with Constant and Heartfree waiting on the jetty for ice-bound ferries, and Lady Fancyfull skating round cut-out trees; *The Sunday Telegraph* (2 November) found John Wood's Brute 'an ageing scarecrow, so fatigued and soured by his debauchery that he has little real heart for it', while Geraldine McEwan and Dorothy Tutin seemed oddly miscast as Lady Brute and Lady Fancyfull. John Retallack's production for the Actors Touring Company, first seen at the Treasurer's House in York on 1 July 1982, came to the Warehouse in London on 14 March 1983; with a cast of seven, many lines were cut, Christine Bishop doubled Bellinda with Madamoiselle, Russell Enoch's Sir John lost his best drunk scene, and Susan Colverd made Lady Fancyfull a figure of horrific pathos. Finally, at the New End on 20 August 1992, Jonathan Best directed a cast of nine, including John Ashton and Corinna Richards as the Brutes, and Jon Harris as a dour, unshaven Constant; *What's On* (26 August) noted one of the wittiest lines as 'I love you more than a Frenchman loves soap'.

NOTE ON THE TEXT

The Provoked Wife was entered in the Term Catalogues for Easter Term 1697, and announced for publication in both the *Post Boy* and the *Post Man* for 11–13 May, about a month after the first performance (Q1). There was a second quarto in 1698 (Q2), a third in 1709 (Q3), and a fourth printing in the first volume of Vanbrugh's collected *Plays* (P) of 1719. Q2 was set up from Q1, Q3 from Q2, and P from Q3. There is no evidence that Vanbrugh supervised the printing of any edition, yet all four are good and the text suffers little contamination in successive printings. Q1 is thus the only edition for which any 'authority' may be claimed; an octavo marked 'LONDON, Printed in the Year 1710' is in fact a Dutch piracy printed at The Hague for Thomas Johnson, who brought out another 'London' edition in 1721.

I have taken as my copy-text the Bodleian Library copy of Q1 (Vet A3.e.682), collated against the British Museum copy (841.d.18), which lacks the final leaf (L3) and binds up the 'Dramatis Personae' before the 'Prologue' and 'Epilogue'. No evidence of press correction was found, although Zimansky reports that seven errors in the Newberry copy of Q1 are corrected in the Lilly Library copy. In my text, all press errors have been silently amended, act and scene divisions regularized, and spelling and capitalization modernized throughout. Punctuation has been modernized wherever the original impedes the sense or flow of Vanbrugh's lines; dashes are used when a speech is broken off, when there is a sudden shift within a single speech from one idea or addressee to another, and when Sir John is drunk. I have modernized the true French spoken by Madamoiselle and Lady Fancyfull, but where Madamoiselle makes fritters of English I have preserved them intact. A few oaths, common phrases, and exclamations have been regularized; thus I gad becomes egad, God b'w'y and good-buy become good-bye, and fe, fi, and fye become fie. 'Aside' appears on the same line as the speech prefix only when the entire speech is so delivered. The copy-text is sparing of stage directions; servants who speak are given entrances but rarely exits, and servants who don't are automatically assumed to be present whenever they are needed. To clarify the action, I have moved some directions to a more appropriate place on the page, and added a few others. All editorial directions are enclosed within square brackets. All substantive departures from the copy-text are glossed, together with interesting rejected variants from the Bodleian Library copies of Q2, Q3, and P.

ABBREVIATIONS

The Provoked Wife

Dobrée	Bonamy Dobrée and Geoffrey Webb, ed., *The Complete Works of Sir John Vanbrugh*, 4 vols. (1927–28).
ed.	editor.
n.s.	new series.
OED	*Oxford English Dictionary*.
P	Collected edition of Vanbrugh's *Plays*, 1719.
PMLA	Publications of the Modern Language Association of America.
Q1	First quarto of 1697.
Q2	Second quarto of 1698.
Q3	Third quarto of 1709.
s.d.	stage direction.
s.p.	speech prefix.
Tilley	M. P. Tilley, *A Dictionary of the Proverbs in England in the Sixteenth and Seventeenth Centuries* (Ann Arbor, 1950).
Zimansky	Curt A. Zimansky, ed., *The Provoked Wife* (1969).

Appendix A

D	Dublin edition of 1743.
L	London edition of Vanbrugh's *Plays*, 1759.

Appendix B

L	London edition of Vanbrugh's *Plays*, 1776.
SM	*A Scotch Medley*, undated broadside.

FURTHER READING

Biography
Laurence Whistler, *Sir John Vanbrugh, Architect and Dramatist: 1664–1726* (1938, rep. 1978).
Kerry Downes, *Sir John Vanbrugh* (1987).

Text
Bonamy Dobrée and Geoffrey Webb, ed., *The Complete Works of Sir John Vanbrugh*, 4 vols. (1927–28). Vol. 1 includes *The Provoked Wife* and *A Short Vindication*.
Frank M. Patterson, 'The revised scenes of *The Provok'd Wife*', *English Language Notes*, 4 (1966–67), 19–23.
Curt A. Zimansky, ed., *The Provoked Wife*, Regents Restoration Drama Series (1969).
Antony Coleman, ed., *The Provoked Wife*, The Revels Plays (Manchester, 1982).
J. C. Ross, 'The printing of Vanbrugh's *The Provok'd Wife* (1697)', *The Library*, Sixth Series, 4 (1982), 397–409.
Michael Cordner, ed., *Sir John Vanbrugh: Four Comedies* (1989).

Stage
The London Stage 1660–1800, ed. W. van Lennep, E. L. Avery, A. H. Scouten, G. Winchester Stone Jnr, and C. B. Hogan (Carbondale, Illinois, 1960–68).
Kalman A. Burnim, *David Garrick, Director* (Pittsburgh, 1961).
Antony Coleman, 'Sir John Brute on the eighteenth century stage', *Restoration and Eighteenth Century Theatre Research*, 8 (1969), 41–46.
The Revels History of Drama in English, V: 1660–1750, ed. John Loftis, Richard Southern, Marion Jones, and A. H. Scouten (1976).
J. L. Styan, *Restoration Comedy in Performance* (1987).

Criticism
Jeremy Collier, *A Short View of the Immorality and Profaneness of the English Stage* (1698).
Sir John Vanbrugh, *A Short Vindication of The Relapse and The Provok'd Wife from Immorality and Prophaneness* (1698).
William Hazlitt, *Lectures on the English Comic Writers* (1819).
Paul Mueschke and Jeannette Fleisher, 'A re-evaluation of Vanbrugh', *PMLA*, 49 (1934), 848–89.

Bernard Harris, *Sir John Vanbrugh*, Writers and their Work, no. 197 (1967).

Lincoln B. Faller, 'Between jest and earnest: the comedy of Sir John Vanbrugh', *Modern Philology*, 72 (1974–75), 17–29.

Arthur R. Huseboe, *Sir John Vanbrugh* (Boston, 1976).

Robert D. Hume, *The Development of English Drama in the Late Seventeenth Century* (Oxford, 1976).

Gerald M. Berkowitz, *Sir John Vanbrugh and the End of Restoration Comedy* (Amsterdam, 1981).

Robert D. Hume, *The Rakish Stage: Studies in English Drama, 1660–1800* (Carbondale, Illinois, 1983).

Michael Cordner, 'Marriage comedy after the 1688 revolution: Southerne to Vanbrugh', *Modern Language Review*, 85 (1990), 273–89.

No place of publication is given for books published solely or jointly in London.

THE

Provok'd Wife :

A

COMEDY,

As it is Acted at the

New Theatre,

IN

Little Lincolns-Inn-Fields.

By the Author of a New Comedy call'd the *Relapse,* or *Virtue in Danger.*

LONDON,
Printed by *J. O.* for *R. Wellington*, at the Lute in St. *Paul's* Church Yard, and *Sam. Briscoe* in *Covent-Garden* 1697.

DRAMATIS PERSONAE

CONSTANT	*Mr Verbruggen*	
HEARTFREE	*Mr Hudson*	
SIR JOHN BRUTE	*Mr Betterton*	
TREBLE, *a singing master*	*Mr Bowman*	
RASOR, *valet de chambre to Sir John Brute*	*Mr Bowen*	5
JUSTICE OF THE PEACE	*Mr Bright*	
LORD RAKE } *companions to Sir John*		
COLONEL BULLY } *Brute*		
CONSTABLE *and* WATCH		
[JO, *a porter*		10
TAILOR		
PAGE *at* 'The Blue Posts'		
FOOTMEN, SERVANTS, *and* DRINKING COMPANIONS *to Lord Rake*]		
LADY BRUTE	*Mrs Barry*	
BELLINDA, *her niece*	*Mrs Bracegirdle*	15
LADY FANCYFULL	*Mrs Bowman*	
MADAMOISELLE	*Mrs Willis*	
CORNET *and* PIPE, *servants to Lady Fancyfull*		
[LOVEWELL, *waiting woman to Lady Brute*]		

17 MADAMOISELLE so spelt in all English editions before 1743

---

19 *waiting woman* A servant who fetches needlework (III.i.14) is more
likely to be a maid than a valet.

PROLOGUE

to *The Provoked Wife*, spoke by Mistress Bracegirdle

Since 'tis the intent and business of the stage,
To copy out the follies of the age;
To hold to every man a faithful glass,
And show him of what species he's an ass;
I hope the next that teaches in the school,   5
Will show our author he's a scribbling fool.
And that the satire may be sure to bite,
Kind heaven, inspire some venomed priest to write,
And grant some ugly lady may indite.
For I would have him lashed, by heavens! I would,   10
Till his presumption swam away in blood.
Three plays at once proclaims a face of brass,
No matter what they are; that's not the case;
To write three plays, e'en that's to be an ass.
But what I least forgive, he knows it too,   15
For to his cost he lately has known you.
Experience shows, to many a writer's smart,
You hold a court where mercy ne'er had part;
So much of the old serpent's sting you have,
You love to damn, as heaven delights to save.   20
In foreign parts, let a bold volunteer
For public good upon the stage appear,
He meets ten thousand smiles to dissipate his fear.
All tickle on th'adventuring young beginner,
And only scourge th'incorrigible sinner;   25
They touch indeed his faults, but with a hand
So gentle, that his merit still may stand;
Kindly they buoy the follies of his pen,
That he may shun 'em when he writes again.

24 *th'* Q1 (the Q2–3, P)

---

8 *venomed priest* prophetic; Jeremy Collier attacked Vanbrugh in *A Short View of the Immorality and Profaneness of the English Stage* (1698)
12 *Three . . . once* Preceding *The Provoked Wife* were *The Relapse* and *I Aesop*, acted in November and December 1696, respectively. Vanbrugh does not count *II Aesop*, a theatrical squib in three scenes, acted in March 1697.
16 *I Aesop* was coolly received.

But 'tis not so in this good-natured town;   30
All's one, an ox, a poet, or a crown:
Old England's play was always knocking down.

THE PROVOKED WIFE

Act I, Scene i

SIR JOHN BRUTE's *House*
Enter SIR JOHN, *solus*

[SIR JOHN]
What cloying meat is love—when matrimony's the sauce to
it! Two years' marriage has debauched my five senses.
Everything I see, everything I hear, everything I feel, everything I smell, and everything I taste—methinks has wife
in't. No boy was ever so weary of his tutor, no girl of her   5
bib, no nun of doing penance, nor old maid of being chaste,
as I am of being married. Sure, there's a secret curse en-
tailed upon the very name of wife. My lady is a young lady,
a fine lady, a witty lady, a virtuous lady—and yet I hate her.
There is but one thing on earth I loathe beyond her; that's   10
fighting. Would my courage come up but to a fourth part of
my ill nature, I'd stand buff to her relations and thrust her
out of doors. But marriage has sunk me down to such an
ebb of resolution, I dare not draw my sword, though even to
get rid of my wife. But here she comes.   15

Enter LADY BRUTE

LADY BRUTE
Do you dine at home today, Sir John?
SIR JOHN
Why, do you expect I should tell you what I don't know
myself?
LADY BRUTE
I thought there was no harm in asking you.
SIR JOHN
If thinking wrong were an excuse for impertinence, women   20
might be justified in most things they say or do.
LADY BRUTE
I'm sorry I have said anything to displease you.

6 *nor* Q1–3 (or P)
12 *stand buff to* stand firm against
22 *I have* Q1–2 (I've Q3, P)

5

SIR JOHN

Sorrow for things past is of as little importance to me, as my
dining at home or abroad ought to be to you.

LADY BRUTE

My enquiry was only that I might have provided what you   25
liked.

SIR JOHN

Six to four you had been in the wrong there again; for what
I liked yesterday I don't like today, and what I like today 'tis
odds I mayn't like tomorrow.

LADY BRUTE

But if I had asked you what you liked?   30

SIR JOHN

Why, then there would have been more asking about it than
the thing was worth.

LADY BRUTE

I wish I did but know how I might please you.

SIR JOHN

Ay, but that sort of knowledge is not a wife's talent.

LADY BRUTE

Whate'er my talent is, I'm sure my will has ever been to   35
make you easy.

SIR JOHN

If women were to have their wills, the world would be finely
governed!

LADY BRUTE

What reason have I given you to use me as you do of late? It
once was otherwise; you married me for love.   40

SIR JOHN

And you me for money; so you have your reward, and I have
mine.

LADY BRUTE

What is it that disturbs you?

SIR JOHN

A parson.

LADY BRUTE

Why, what has he done to you?   45

SIR JOHN

He has married me.   (*Exit* SIR JOHN)

LADY BRUTE (*Sola*)

The devil's in the fellow, I think!—I was told before I

---

31 *have been* Q1–3 (be P)
32 *was* Q1–3 (is P)
47 s.p. LADY BRUTE (*Sola*) Q2–3, P (*Enter Lady* Brute, *sola* Q1)

married him that thus 'twould be. But I thought I had
charms enough to govern him, and that where there was an
estate a woman must needs be happy; so my vanity has   50
deceived me, and my ambition has made me uneasy. But
some comfort still; if one would be revenged of him, these
are good times; a woman may have a gallant and a separate
maintenance too. —The surly puppy!—Yet he's a fool for't,
for hitherto he has been no monster. But who knows how   55
far he may provoke me? I never loved him, yet I have been
ever true to him; and that, in spite of all the attacks of art
and nature upon a poor weak woman's heart in favour of
a tempting lover. Methinks so noble a defence as I have
made should be rewarded with a better usage.—Or who can   60
tell?—Perhaps a good part of what I suffer from my husband
may be a judgment upon me for my cruelty to my lover.—
Lord, with what pleasure could I indulge that thought,
were there but a possibility of finding arguments to make it
good!—And how do I know but there may? Let me see.—   65
What opposes? My matrimonial vow.—Why, what did I
vow? I think I promised to be true to my husband. Well;
and he promised to be kind to me. But he han't kept his
word.—Why then, I'm absolved from mine. Ay, that seems
clear to me. The argument's good between the king and the   70
people, why not between the husband and the wife?—Oh,
but that condition was not expressed.—No matter; 'twas
understood. Well, by all I see, if I argue the matter a little
longer with myself, I shan't find so many bugbears in the
way as I thought I should. Lord, what fine notions of   75
virtue do we women take up upon the credit of old foolish
philosophers! Virtue's its own reward, virtue's this, virtue's
that—virtue's an ass, and a gallant's worth forty on't.

Enter BELLINDA

Good morrow, dear cousin.
BELLINDA
Good morrow, madam; you look pleased this morning.   80
LADY BRUTE
  I am so.

55 *monster* cuckold

53-4 *gallant . . . too* An adulteress legally separated from her husband's
  'bed and board' was entitled to alimony, but could not marry her
  gallant.
70-1 *The . . . people* Lady Brute recalls the social contract realized in the
  constitutional settlements of 1689; if James II violates his coronation
  vows, the people are absolved from their oath of allegiance.

BELLINDA
With what, pray?

LADY BRUTE
With my husband.

BELLINDA
Drown husbands! for yours is a provoking fellow. As he
went out just now, I prayed him to tell me what time of day   85
'twas; and he asked me if I took him for the church clock,
that was obliged to tell all the parish.

LADY BRUTE
He has been saying some good obliging things to me too. In
short, Bellinda, he has used me so barbarously of late that I
could almost resolve to play the downright wife—and   90
cuckold him.

BELLINDA
That would be downright indeed.

LADY BRUTE
Why, after all, there's more to be said for't than you'd
imagine, child. I know, according to the strict statute law of
religion, I should do wrong; but if there were a Court of   95
Chancery in heaven, I'm sure I should cast him.

BELLINDA
If there were a House of Lords you might.

LADY BRUTE
In either I should infallibly carry my cause. Why, he is the
first aggressor. Not I.

BELLINDA
Ay, but you know, we must return good for evil.   100

LADY BRUTE
That may be a mistake in the translation.—Prithee be of my
opinion, Bellinda, for I'm positive I'm in the right; and if
you'll keep up the prerogative of a woman, you'll likewise
be positive you are in the right, whenever you do anything
you have a mind to. But I shall play the fool and jest on, till   105
I make you begin to think I'm in earnest.

---

96 *cast him* defeat him in an action at law

95-6 *Court of Chancery* an equity court moderating the rigour of the law
by reference to general principles of justice, and giving relief in cases
where the common-law courts provide no remedy; it did not usually
deal with divorce

97 *House of Lords* A complete divorce, leaving both partners free to
remarry, could be obtained only by passing a private bill through
Parliament and up to the royal assent; the first such divorce was granted
in April 1698.

BELLINDA

I shan't take the liberty, madam, to think of anything that
you desire to keep a secret from me.

LADY BRUTE

Alas, my dear, I have no secrets. My heart could never yet
confine my tongue.   110

BELLINDA

Your eyes, you mean; for I am sure I have seen them
gadding, when your tongue has been locked up safe enough.

LADY BRUTE

My eyes gadding! Prithee after who, child?

BELLINDA

Why, after one that thinks you hate him, as much as I know
you love him.   115

LADY BRUTE

Constant, you mean.

BELLINDA

I do so.

LADY BRUTE

Lord, what should put such a thing into your head?

BELLINDA

That which puts things into most people's heads, ob-
servation.   120

LADY BRUTE

Why, what have you observed, in the name of wonder?

BELLINDA

I have observed you blush when you meet him, force yourself away from him, and then be out of humour with
everything about you. In a word, never was poor creature
so spurred on by desire, and so reined in with fear!   125

LADY BRUTE

How strong is fancy!

BELLINDA

How weak is woman!

LADY BRUTE

Prithee, niece, have a better opinion of your aunt's inclinations.

BELLINDA

Dear aunt, have a better opinion of your niece's under-   130
standing.

LADY BRUTE

You'll make me angry.

122 *meet* Q1–3 (met P)
128–9 *inclinations* Q1–2 (inclination Q3, P)

BELLINDA
You'll make me laugh.

LADY BRUTE
Then you are resolved to persist?

BELLINDA
Positively.   135

LADY BRUTE
And all I can say—

BELLINDA
Will signify nothing.

LADY BRUTE
Though I should swear 'twere false—

BELLINDA
I should think it true.

LADY BRUTE
Then let us both forgive (*Kissing her*), for we have both   140
offended: I in making a secret, you in discovering it.

BELLINDA
Good nature may do much; but you have more reason to
forgive one, than I have to pardon t'other.

LADY BRUTE
'Tis true, Bellinda, you have given me so many proofs of
your friendship, that my reserve has been indeed a crime.   145
But that you may more easily forgive me, remember, child,
that when our nature prompts us to a thing our honour and
religion have forbid us, we would (were't possible) conceal,
even from the soul itself, the knowledge of the body's
weakness.   150

BELLINDA
Well, I hope, to make your friend amends, you'll hide
nothing from her for the future, though the body should
still grow weaker and weaker.

LADY BRUTE
No, from this moment I have no more reserve; and for a
proof of my repentance, I own, Bellinda, I'm in danger.   155
Merit and wit assault me from without; nature and love
solicit me within; my husband's barbarous usage piques me
to revenge; and Satan, catching at the fair occasion, throws
in my way that vengeance which, of all vengeance, pleases
women best.   160

BELLINDA
'Tis well Constant don't know the weakness of the forti-
fications; for o'my conscience he'd soon come on to the
assault.

LADY BRUTE

Ay, and I'm afraid carry the town too. But whatever you may have observed, I have dissembled so well as to keep 165 him ignorant. So you see I'm no coquette, Bellinda; and if you'll follow my advice you'll never be one neither. 'Tis true, coquetry is one of the main ingredients in the natural composition of a woman, and I, as well as others, could be well enough pleased to see a crowd of young fellows, ogling 170 and glancing and watching all occasions to do forty foolish officious things; nay, should some of 'em push on, even to hanging or drowning. Why—faith—if I should let pure woman alone, I should e'en be but too well pleased with't.

BELLINDA

I'll swear 'twould tickle me strangely. 175

LADY BRUTE

But, after all, 'tis a vicious practice in us, to give the least encouragement but where we design to come to a conclusion. For 'tis an unreasonable thing, to engage a man in a disease which we beforehand resolve we never will apply a cure to. 180

BELLINDA

'Tis true; but then a woman must abandon one of the supreme blessings of her life. For I am fully convinced, no man has half that pleasure in possessing a mistress, as a woman has in jilting a gallant.

LADY BRUTE

The happiest woman then on earth must be our neighbour. 185

BELLINDA

Oh, the impertinent composition! She has vanity and affectation enough to make her a ridiculous original, in spite of all that art and nature ever furnished to any of her sex before her.

LADY BRUTE

She concludes all men her captives; and whatever course 190 they take, it serves to confirm her in that opinion.

BELLINDA

If they shun her, she thinks 'tis modesty, and takes it for a proof of their passion.

---

167 *you'll follow* Q1-3 (you follow P)
174 *woman* Q1-3 (women P)
186 *impertinent* incongruous, absurd
187 *original* eccentric

LADY BRUTE

And if they are rude to her, 'tis conduct, and done to prevent
town-talk.   195

BELLINDA

When her folly makes 'em laugh, she thinks they are pleased
with her wit.

LADY BRUTE

And when her impertinence makes 'em dull, concludes they
are jealous of her favours.

BELLINDA

All their actions and their words, she takes for granted, aim   200
at her.

LADY BRUTE

And pities all other women, because she thinks they envy
her.

BELLINDA

Pray, out of pity to ourselves, let us find a better subject, for
I am weary of this. Do you think your husband inclined to   205
jealousy?

LADY BRUTE

Oh, no; he does not love me well enough for that. Lord,
how wrong men's maxims are! They are seldom jealous of
their wives, unless they are very fond of 'em; whereas they
ought to consider the women's inclinations, for there   210
depends their fate. Well, men may talk; but they are not so
wise as we—that's certain.

BELLINDA

At least in our affairs.

LADY BRUTE

Nay, I believe we should outdo 'em in the business of the
state, too; for methinks they do and undo, and make but   215
mad work on't.

BELLINDA

Why then don't we get into the intrigues of government as
well as they?

LADY BRUTE

Because we have intrigues of our own that make us more
sport, child. And so let's in and consider of 'em.   (*Exeunt*)   220

194 *conduct* discretion
205 *I am* Q1–2 (I'm Q3, P)
210 *women's* Q2–3, P (woman's Q1)
216 *mad* Q1 (bad Q2–3, P)

Act I, Scene ii

A dressing room
Enter LADY FANCYFULL, MADAMOISELLE, *and* CORNET

LADY FANCYFULL
How do I look this morning?
CORNET
Your ladyship looks very ill, truly.
LADY FANCYFULL
Lard, how ill-natured thou art, Cornet, to tell me so, though
the thing should be true. Don't you know that I have
humility enough to be but too easily out of conceit with   5
myself? Hold the glass; I dare swear that will have more
manners than you have.—Madamoiselle, let me have your
opinion too.
MADAMOISELLE
My opinion pe, matam, dat your ladyship never look so well
in your life.   10
LADY FANCYFULL
Well, the French are the prettiest obliging people; they say
the most acceptable, well-mannered things—and never
flatter.
MADAMOISELLE
Your ladyship say great justice inteed.
LADY FANCYFULL
Nay, everything's just in my house but Cornet. The very   15
looking-glass gives her the *démenti*. (*Looking affectedly in the
glass*) But I'm almost afraid it flatters me, it makes me look
so very engaging.
MADAMOISELLE
Inteed, matam, your face pe hansomer den all de looking-
glass in tee world, *croyez-moi*!   20
LADY FANCYFULL
But is it possible my eyes can be so languishing—and so
very full of fire?
MADAMOISELLE
Matam, if de glass was burning-glass, I believe your eyes
set de fire in de house.
LADY FANCYFULL
You may take that night-gown, Madamoiselle.—Get out of   25

16 *démenti* lie
20 *croyez-moi*! believe me!

the room, Cornet! I can't endure you. (*Exit* CORNET) This
wench, methinks, does look so unsufferably ugly.

MADAMOISELLE

Everyting look ugly, matam, dat stand by your latiship.

LADY FANCYFULL

No, really, Madamoiselle—methinks you look mighty
pretty.   30

MADAMOISELLE

Ah, matam! de moon have no *éclat* ven de sun appear.

LADY FANCYFULL

O pretty expression! Have you ever been in love, Madamoiselle?

MADAMOISELLE (*Sighing*)

Oui, matam.

LADY FANCYFULL

And were you beloved again?   35

MADAMOISELLE (*Sighing*)

No, matam.

LADY FANCYFULL

O ye gods! What an unfortunate creature should I be in such
a case! But nature has made me nice for my own defence:
I'm nice, strangely nice, Madamoiselle; I believe were the
merit of whole mankind bestowed upon one single person,   40
I should still think the fellow wanted something to make
it worth my while to take notice of him. And yet I could
love—nay, fondly love—were it possible to have a thing
made on purpose for me: for I'm not cruel, Madamoiselle,
I'm only nice.   45

MADAMOISELLE

Ah, matam, I wish I was fine gentelman for your sake. I do
all de ting in de world to get leetel way into your heart. I
make song, I make verse, I give you de serenade, I give great
many present to Madamoiselle; I no eat, I no sleep, I be
lean, I be mad, I hang myself, I drown myself. *Ah, ma chère*   50
dame, que je vous aimerais!   (*Embracing her*)

LADY FANCYFULL

Well, the French have strange obliging ways with 'em; you
may take those two pair of gloves, Madamoiselle.

---

26 s.d. (*Exit* CORNET) Q1 prints this after Lady Fancyfull's line (*omitted*
   Q2–3, P)
31 *éclat* brightness
35 *you beloved* Q2–3, P (you, beloved Q1) Dobrée thinks the pause
   intentional
50–1 *Ah . . . aimerais!* Ah, my dear lady, how I would love you!

MADAMOISELLE
Me humbly tanke my sweet lady.

Enter CORNET

CORNET
Madam, here's a letter for your ladyship by the penny-post.   55
                                                        [*Exit*]
LADY FANCYFULL
Some new conquest, I'll warrant you. For, without vanity,
I looked extremely clear last night, when I went to the
Park.—Oh, agreeable! Here's a new song made of me. And
ready set, too! Oh, thou welcome thing! (*Kissing it*)—Call
Pipe hither; she shall sing it instantly.   60

Enter PIPE

Here, sing me this new song, Pipe.

SONG
I

[PIPE]   Fly, fly, you happy shepherds, fly,
               Avoid Philira's charms;
           The rigour of her heart denies
               The heaven that's in her arms.   65
           Ne'er hope to gaze, and then retire,
               Nor yielding, to be blest:
           Nature, who formed her eyes of fire,
               Of ice composed her breast.
II
           Yet, lovely maid, this once believe   70
               A slave, whose zeal you move;
           The gods, alas, your youth deceive,
               Their heaven consists in love.
           In spite of all the thanks you owe,
               You may reproach 'em this: 75
           That where they did their form bestow
               They have denied their bliss.   [*Exit*]

LADY FANCYFULL
Well, there may be faults, Madamoiselle, but the design is so

57 *clear* of fresh complexion, blooming
73 *Their* Q1, P (The Q2–3)

55 *penny-post* collected and delivered every two hours in town
58 *Park* St James's Park, a fashionable promenade and lovers' rendezvous

very obliging 'twould be a matchless ingratitude in me to
discover 'em.   80

MADAMOISELLE
Ma foi, matam, I tink de gentelman's song tell you de trute.
If you never love, you never be happy.—*Ah, que j'aime
l'amour, moi!*

Enter SERVANT, *with another letter*

SERVANT
Madam, here's another letter for your ladyship.   [*Exit*]

LADY FANCYFULL
'Tis thus I am importuned every morning, Madamoiselle.   85
Pray, how do the French ladies when they are thus
accablées?

MADAMOISELLE
Matam, dey never complain. *Au contraire!* When one Frense
laty have got hundred lover, den she do all she can—to get
hundred more.   90

LADY FANCYFULL
Well, strike me dead, I think they have *le goût bon*! For 'tis an
unutterable pleasure to be adored by all the men and envied
by all the women.—Yet I'll swear I'm concerned at the
torture I give 'em. Lard, why was I formed to make the
whole creation uneasy?—But let me read my letter. (*Reads*)   95
'If you have a mind to hear of your faults, instead of being
praised for your virtues, take the pains to walk in the Green
Walk in St James's with your woman an hour hence.
You'll there meet one who hates you for some things, as he
could love you for others, and therefore is willing to en-   100
deavour your reformation.—If you come to the place I
mention, you'll know who I am; if you don't, you never
shall: so take your choice'.—This is strangely familiar,
Madamoiselle; now have I a provoking fancy to know who
this impudent fellow is.   105

MADAMOISELLE
Den take your scarf and your mask, and go to de rendezvous. De Frense laty do *justement comme ça*.

81 *Ma foi* Upon my soul
82-3 *Ah . . . moi!* Ah, I like love, I do!
87 *accablées* overwhelmed, snowed under
88 *Au contraire!* On the contrary!
91 *le goût bon* good taste
107 *justement comme ça* exactly like that

97-8 *Green Walk* a long avenue of lime trees ending in a knot of elms

LADY FANCYFULL
Rendezvous! What, rendezvous with a man, Madamoiselle!
MADAMOISELLE
Eh, pourquoi non?
LADY FANCYFULL
What, and a man perhaps I never saw in my life!   110
MADAMOISELLE
Tant mieux; c'est donc quelque chose de nouveau.
LADY FANCYFULL
Why, how do I know what designs he may have? He may
intend to ravish me, for aught I know.
MADAMOISELLE
Ravish?—Bagatelle! I would fain see one impudent rogue
ravish Madamoiselle! *Oui, je le voudrais.*   115
LADY FANCUFULL
Oh, but my reputation, Madamoiselle, my reputation! *Ah,
ma chère réputation!*
MADAMOISELLE
Matam, *quand on l'a une fois perdue, on n'en est plus embar-
rassée.*
LADY FANCYFULL
Fie, Madamoiselle, fie! Reputation is a jewel.   120
MADAMOISELLE
—*Qui coûte bien cher*, matam.
LADY FANCYFULL
Why, sure you would not sacrifice your honour to your
pleasure?
MADAMOISELLE
Je suis philosophe.
LADY FANCYFULL
Bless me, how you talk! Why, what if honour be a burden,   125
Madamoiselle, must it not be borne?

---

109 *Eh, pourquoi non?* Well, why not?
111 *Tant ... nouveau* All the better; then it will be an entirely new
    experience
115 *Oui, je le voudrais* Yes, I would indeed
116–17 *Ah ... réputation!* Ah, my dear reputation!
118–19 *quand ... embarrassée* once you have lost it, you no longer have it
    to worry about
121 *cher* ed. (chère Q1–3, P, but *jewel*, i.e. *bijou* or *joyau*, is masculine)
121 *Qui ... cher* And a very expensive one
124 *Je suis philosophe* I am resigned to the inevitable

MADAMOISELLE

Chacun à sa façon. Quand quelque chose m'incommode, moi, je m'en défais, vite.

LADY FANCYFULL

Get you gone, you little naughty Frenchwoman you! I vow and swear I must turn you out of doors, if you talk thus.   130

MADAMOISELLE

Turn me out of doors! Turn yourself out of doors and go see what de gentleman have to say to you!—*Tenez.*—(*Giving her her things hastily*) *Voilà votre écharpe, voilà votre coiffe, voilà votre masque, voilà tout!*—(*Calling within*) Hey, Mercure! *Coquin,* call one chair for matam, and one oder for me.   135
Va-t'en vite!—(*Turning to her lady, and helping her on hastily with her things*) *Allons,* matam; *dépêchez-vous donc. Mon Dieu, quels scrupules!*

LADY FANCYFULL

Well, for once, Madamoiselle, I'll follow your advice, out of the intemperate desire I have to know who this ill-bred   140
fellow is. But I have too much *délicatesse* to make a practice on it.

MADAMOISELLE

Belle chose vraiment que la délicatesse, lors qu'il s'agit de se divertir!—Ah, çà!—Vous voilà équipée; partons.—Hé bien!—qu'avez vous donc?   145

LADY FANCYFULL

J'ai peur.

MADAMOISELLE

Je n'en ai point, moi.

127–8 *Chacun . . . vite* Each in his own way. When something is a nuisance to me, I get rid of it, quickly.

132–4 *Tenez . . . tout!* There . . . Here's your scarf, here's your hood, here's your mask. That's everything!

135 *Coquin* You rascal

136–8 *Va-t'en . . . scrupules!* Go quickly! . . . Come along, matam; make haste. Heavens, what scruples!

138 *quels* ed. (quelles Q1–3, P)

141 *délicatesse* delicacy

143–7 *Belle . . . moi* 'A fine thing, delicacy, when you are out to enjoy yourself!—Now then!—You're all dressed up; let's go.—Well, what's the matter?' 'I'm frightened'. 'I'm not'.

---

135 *Coquin* may be a proper name, for Q1 does not distinguish French words by italics; but one man can call two sedan-chairs by himself, particularly when he is named after the Roman god of roads and rascals, or *coquins*.

LADY FANCYFULL
    I dare not go.
MADAMOISELLE
    Demeurez donc.
LADY FANCYFULL
    Je suis poltrone.   150
MADAMOISELLE
    Tant pis pour vous.
LADY FANCYFULL
    Curiosity's a wicked devil.
MADAMOISELLE
    C'est une charmante sainte.
LADY FANCYFULL
    It ruined our first parents.
MADAMOISELLE
    Elle a bien diverti leurs enfants.   155
LADY FANCYFULL
    L'honneur est contre.
MADAMOISELLE
    Le plaisir est pour.
LADY FANCYFULL
    Must I then go?
MADAMOISELLE
    Must you go?—Must you eat, must you drink, must you
    sleep, must you live? De nature bid you do one; de nature   160
    bid you do t'oder. *Vous me ferez enrager!*
LADY FANCYFULL
    But when reason corrects nature, Madamoiselle?
MADAMOISELLE
    Elle est donc bien insolente; c'est sa soeur aînée.
LADY FANCYFULL
    Do you then prefer your nature to your reason, Mada-
    moiselle?   165
MADAMOISELLE
    Oui-dà!
LADY FANCYFULL
    Pourquoi?

149–51 *Demeurez ... vous* 'Don't go then'. 'I'm a coward'. 'The more fool
    you'.
153 *C'est ... sainte* It's a charming saint
155–7 *Elle ... pour* 'It has given a lot of fun to their children'. 'Honour is
    against it'. 'Pleasure is for it'.
161 *Vous ... enrager!* You are driving me mad!
163 *Elle ... aînée* Then she presumes too much; nature is her elder sister
166–7 *Oui-dà! Pourquoi?* 'Yes indeed!' 'Why?'

MADAMOISELLE
Because my nature make me merry, my reason make me sad.
LADY FANCYFULL
Ah, la méchante Française!
MADAMOISELLE
Ah, la belle Anglaise!   ([*Exit,*] *forcing her lady off*)   170

Act II, Scene i

St James's Park
Enter LADY FANCYFULL *and* MADAMOISELLE

LADY FANCYFULL
Well, I vow, Madamoiselle, I'm strangely impatient to
know who this confident fellow is.

Enter HEARTFREE

Look, there's Heartfree. But sure it can't be him; he's a
professed woman-hater. Yet who knows what my wicked
eyes may have done?   5
MADAMOISELLE
Il nous approche, madame.
LADY FANCYFULL
Yes, 'tis he; now will he be most intolerably cavalier, though
he should be in love with me.
HEARTFREE
Madam, I'm your humble servant; I perceive you have more
humility and good nature than I thought you had.   10
LADY FANCYFULL
What you attribute to humility and good nature, sir, may
perhaps be only due to curiosity. I had a mind to know who
'twas had ill manners enough to write that letter.
        (*Throwing him his letter*)
HEARTFREE
Well; and now, I hope, you are satisfied.
LADY FANCYFULL
I am so, sir; good-bye to ye.   [*Going*]   15

168 *sad* ed. (mad Q1–3, P)
169–70 *Ah . . . Anglaise!* 'Ah, this wicked Frenchwoman!' 'Ah, this beautiful
        Englishwoman!'
170 s.d. *forcing . . . off* Q1 follows this with 'The End of the first Act'.
  6 *madame* ed. (madam Q1–3, P)
  6 *Il . . . madame* He is approaching us, madam

HEARTFREE

Nay, hold there! though you have done your business, I
han't done mine; by your ladyship's leave, we must have
one moment's prattle together. Have you a mind to be the
prettiest woman about town, or not?—How she stares upon
me!—What! this passes for an impertinent question with   20
you now, because you think you are so already.

LADY FANCYFULL

Pray, sir, let me ask you a question in my turn: by what
right do you pretend to examine me?

HEARTFREE

By the same right that the strong govern the weak, because
I have you in my power; for you cannot get so quickly to   25
your coach but I shall have time enough to make you hear
everything I have to say to you.

LADY FANCYFULL

These are strange liberties you take, Mr Heartfree!

HEARTFREE

They are so, madam, but there's no help for it; for know,
that I have a design upon you.   30

LADY FANCYFULL

Upon me, sir!

HEARTFREE

Yes; and one that will turn to your glory and my comfort,
if you will but be a little wiser than you use to be.

LADY FANCYFULL

Very well, sir.

HEARTFREE

Let me see.—Your vanity, madam, I take to be about some   . 35
eight degrees higher than any woman's in the town, let
t'other be who she will; and my indifference is naturally
about the same pitch. Now, could you find the way to turn
this indifference into fire and flames, methinks your vanity
ought to be satisfied; and this, perhaps, you might bring   40
about upon pretty reasonable terms.

LADY FANCYFULL

And pray, at what rate would this indifference be bought
off, if one should have so depraved an appetite to desire it?

HEARTFREE

Why, madam, to drive a Quaker's bargain and make but
one word with you, if I do part with it, you must lay me   45
down—your affectation.

44–5 *Quaker's ... word* By trading at fixed prices Quakers reduced bar-
gaining to a single word: yea or nay.

LADY FANCYFULL
My affectation, sir!
HEARTFREE
Why, I ask you nothing but what you may very well spare.
LADY FANCYFULL
You grow rude, sir.—Come, Madamoiselle, 'tis high time
to be gone.   50
MADAMOISELLE
Allons, allons, allons!
HEARTFREE (*Stopping 'em*)
Nay, you may as well stand still; for hear me you shall,
walk which way you please.
LADY FANCYFULL
What mean you, sir?
HEARTFREE
I mean to tell you, that you are the most ungrateful woman   55
upon earth.
LADY FANCYFULL
Ungrateful! To who?
HEARTFREE
To nature.
LADY FANCYFULL
Why, what has nature done for me?
HEARTFREE
What you have undone by art. It made you handsome; it   60
gave you beauty to a miracle, a shape without a fault, wit
enough to make 'em relish, and so turned you loose to your
own discretion; which has made such work with you, that
you are become the pity of our sex and the jest of your
own. There is not a feature in your face but you have found   65
the way to teach it some affected convulsion; your feet,
your hands, your very fingers' ends, are directed never to
move without some ridiculous air or other; and your
language is a suitable trumpet, to draw people's eyes upon
the raree-show.   70
MADAMOISELLE (*Aside*)
Est-ce qu'on fait l'amour en Angleterre comme ça?
LADY FANCYFULL (*Aside*)
Now could I cry for madness, but that I know he'd laugh at
me for it.

51 *Allons, allons, allons!* Come along, come along, let's be off!
52 s.d. *'em* Q1–3 (them P)
71 *Est-ce . . . ça?* Is that how they pay court in England?

70 *raree-show* a peep-show hawked round the streets in a box

HEARTFREE

Now do you hate me for telling you the truth, but that's
because you don't believe it is so; for were you once con-   75
vinced of that, you'd reform for your own sake. But 'tis as
hard to persuade a woman to quit anything that makes her
ridiculous, as 'tis to prevail with a poet to see a fault in his
own play.

LADY FANCYFULL

Every circumstance of nice breeding must needs appear   80
ridiculous to one who has so natural an antipathy to good
manners.

HEARTFREE

But suppose I could find the means to convince you that
the whole world is of my opinion? and that those who flatter
and commend you do it to no other intent but to make you   85
persevere in your folly, that they may continue in their
mirth?

LADY FANCYFULL

Sir, though you and all that world you talk of should be so
impertinently officious as to think to persuade me I don't
know how to behave myself, I should still have charity   90
enough for my own understanding to believe myself in the
right, and all you in the wrong.

MADAMOISELLE

Le voilà mort! (*Exeunt* LADY FANCYFULL *and* MADAMOISELLE)

HEARTFREE (*Gazing after her*)

There her single clapper has published the sense of the
whole sex!—Well, this once I have endeavoured to wash   95
the blackamoor white; but henceforward I'll sooner undertake to teach sincerity to a courtier, generosity to an usurer,
honesty to a lawyer, nay, humility to a divine, than discretion to a woman I see has once set her heart upon playing
the fool.   100

Enter CONSTANT

'Morrow, Constant.

CONSTANT

Good morrow, Jack; what are you doing here this morning?

HEARTFREE

Doing! Guess, if thou canst.—Why, I have been endeavour-
ing to persuade my Lady Fancyfull that she's the foolishest
woman about town.   105

93 *Le voilà mort!* That's done for him!
94 *clapper* tongue

CONSTANT
A pretty endeavour, truly!

HEARTFREE
I have told her, in as plain English as I could speak, both
what the town says of her and what I think of her. In short,
I have used her as an absolute king would do Magna Charta.

CONSTANT
And how does she take it?   110

HEARTFREE
As children do pills; bite 'em, but can't swallow 'em.

CONSTANT
But, prithee, what has put it in your head, of all mankind,
to turn reformer?

HEARTFREE
Why, one thing was, the morning hung upon my hands—I
did not know what to do with myself; and another was, that   115
as little as I care for women, I could not see with patience
one that heaven had taken such wondrous pains about, be
so very industrious to make herself the jack-pudding of the
creation.

CONSTANT
Well, now could I almost wish to see my cruel mistress   120
make the selfsame use of what heaven has done for her, that
so I might be cured of a disease that makes me so very
uneasy; for love, love is the devil, Heartfree.

HEARTFREE
And why do you let the devil govern you?

CONSTANT
Because I have more flesh and blood than grace and self-   125
denial. My dear, dear mistress!—'Sdeath! that so genteel a
woman should be a saint, when religion's out of fashion!

HEARTFREE
Nay, she's much in the wrong, truly; but who knows how
far time and good example may prevail?

112 *in* Q1–2 (into Q3, P)
118 *jack-pudding* laughing-stock

---

109 *as ... Charta* i.e., without respect; only constitutional monarchs
    honour charters setting down their people's rights
118 *jack-pudding* Jack Puddings were fairground drolls who 'commit such
    Blunders and Mistakes in every Step they take, and every Word they
    utter, as those who listen to them would be ashamed of' (the *Spectator*,
    no. 47, 24 April 1711).

CONSTANT

Oh, they have played their parts in vain already. 'Tis now   130
two years since that damned fellow her husband invited me
to his wedding; and there was the first time I saw that
charming woman, whom I have loved ever since more than
e'er a martyr did his soul; but she's cold, my friend, still
cold as the northern star.   135

HEARTFREE

So are all women by nature, which makes 'em so willing to
be warmed.

CONSTANT

Oh, don't profane the sex! Prithee think 'em all angels for
her sake, for she's virtuous even to a fault.

HEARTFREE

A lover's head is a good accountable thing truly! He adores 140
his mistress for being virtuous, and yet is very angry with
her because she won't be lewd.

CONSTANT

Well, the only relief I expect in my misery is to see thee
some day or other as deeply engaged as myself, which will
force me to be merry in the midst of all my misfortunes.   145

HEARTFREE

That day will never come, be assured, Ned. Not but that I
can pass a night with a woman, and for the time, perhaps,
make myself as good sport as you can do. Nay, I can court
a woman too, call her nymph, angel, goddess—what you
please. But here's the difference 'twixt you and I: I persuade 150
a woman she's an angel; she persuades you she's one.—
Prithee, let me tell you how I avoid falling in love; that
which serves me for prevention, may chance to serve you
for a cure.

CONSTANT

Well, use the ladies moderately then, and I'll hear you.   155

HEARTFREE

That using 'em moderately undoes us all; but I'll use 'em
justly, and that you ought to be satisfied with.—I always
consider a woman, not as the tailor, the shoemaker, the tire-
woman, the sempstress, and (which is more than all that)
the poet makes her; but I consider her as pure nature has   160

136 *'em* Q1–3 (them P)
138 *'em* Q1–3 (them P)
151 *she* Q1–2 (and she Q3, P)
158–9 *tire-woman* dressmaker
159 *and (which* Q3, P (and which Q1–2)

contrived her, and that more strictly than I should have done our old grandmother Eve, had I seen her naked in the garden; for I consider her turned inside out. Her heart well examined, I find there pride, vanity, covetousness, indiscretion, but above all things—malice: plots eternally   165
a-forging to destroy one another's reputations, and as honestly to charge the levity of men's tongues with the scandal; hourly debates how to make poor gentlemen in love with 'em, with no other intent but to use 'em like dogs when they have done; a constant desire of doing more   170
mischief, and an everlasting war waged against truth and good nature.

CONSTANT
Very well, sir; an admirable composition truly!

HEARTFREE
Then for her outside, I consider it merely as an outside; she has a thin tiffany covering over just such stuff as you and   175
I are made on. As for her motion, her mien, her airs, and all those tricks, I know they affect you mightily. If you should see your mistress at a coronation, dragging her peacock's train with all her state and insolence about her, 'twould strike you with all the awful thoughts that heaven itself   180
could pretend to from you; whereas I turn the whole matter into a jest, and suppose her strutting in the selfsame stately manner, with nothing on but her stays and her under scanty quilted petticoat.

CONSTANT
Hold thy profane tongue! for I'll hear no more.   185

HEARTFREE
What, you'll love on, then?

CONSTANT
Yes, to eternity.

HEARTFREE
Yet you have no hopes at all?

CONSTANT
None.

HEARTFREE
Nay, the resolution may be discreet enough; perhaps you   190
have found out some new philosophy—that love's like virtue, its own reward: so you and your mistress will be as well content at a distance, as others that have less learning are in coming together.

---

175 *tiffany* a kind of transparent silk
183–4 *under . . . petticoat* a short padded underskirt of coarse cloth

CONSTANT

No; but if she should prove kind at last, my dear Heartfree!   195
(*Embracing him*)

HEARTFREE

Nay, prithee, don't take me for your mistress, for lovers
are very troublesome.

CONSTANT

Well, who knows what time may do?

HEARTFREE

—And just now he was sure time could do nothing!

CONSTANT

Yet not one kind glance in two years is somewhat strange.   200

HEARTFREE

Not strange at all: she don't like you, that's all the business.

CONSTANT

Prithee don't distract me!

HEARTFREE

Nay, you are a good handsome young fellow; she might use
you better. Come, will you go see her? Perhaps she may
have changed her mind; there's some hopes as long as she's   205
a woman.

CONSTANT

Oh, 'tis in vain to visit her! Sometimes to get a sight of her I
visit that beast her husband, but she certainly finds some
pretence to quit the room as soon as I enter.

HEARTFREE

It's much she don't tell him you have made love to her, too,   210
for that's another good-natured thing usual amongst women,
in which they have several ends. Sometimes 'tis to recommend their virtue, that they may be lewd with the greater
security. Sometimes 'tis to make their husbands fight, in
hopes they may be killed when their affairs require it should   215
be so. But most commonly 'tis to engage two men in a
quarrel, that they may have the credit of being fought for;
and if the lover's killed in the business, they cry 'Poor
fellow! he had ill luck'—and so they go to cards.

CONSTANT

Thy injuries to women are not to be forgiven. Look to't, if   220
ever thou dost fall into their hands—

HEARTFREE

They can't use me worse than they do you, that speak well
of 'em.—O ho! here comes the knight.

Enter SIR JOHN BRUTE

Your humble servant, Sir John.

SIR JOHN
    Servant, sir.   225
HEARTFREE
    How does all your family?
SIR JOHN
    Pox o'my family!
CONSTANT
    How does your lady? I han't seen her abroad a good while.
SIR JOHN
    Do! I don't know how she does, not I. She was well enough
    yesterday; I han't been home tonight.   230
CONSTANT
    What, were you out of town?
SIR JOHN
    Out of town! no, I was drinking.
CONSTANT
    You are a true Englishman; don't know your own happiness.
    If I were married to such a woman, I would not be from
    her a night for all the wine in France.   235
SIR JOHN
    Not from her!—Oons! what a time should a man have of
    that!
HEARTFREE
    Why, there's no division, I hope?
SIR JOHN
    No; but there's a conjunction, and that's worse; a pox o'the
    parson!—Why the plague don't you two marry? I fancy I   240
    look like the devil to you.
HEARTFREE
    Why, you don't think you have horns, do you?
SIR JOHN
    No; I believe my wife's religion will keep her honest.
HEARTFREE
    And what will make her keep her religion?
SIR JOHN
    Persecution; and therefore she shall have it.   245
HEARTFREE
    Have a care, knight! women are tender things.
SIR JOHN
    And yet, methinks, 'tis a hard matter to break their hearts.

230 *tonight* last night; apparently a day passes between I.i and I.ii
236 *Oons* a corruption of *God's wounds*
239 *o'the* Q1–2 (of the Q3, P)

239 *conjunction* the concourse of two planets in the same degree of the
    zodiac; in astrology, generally malign

CONSTANT

Fie, fie! You have one of the best wives in the world, and yet
you seem the most uneasy husband.

SIR JOHN

Best wives!—The woman's well enough, she has no vice that   250
I know of, but she's a wife, and—Damn a wife! If I were
married to a hogshead of claret, matrimony would make me
hate it.

HEARTFREE

Why did you marry, then? You were old enough to know
your own mind.   255

SIR JOHN

Why did I marry? I married because I had a mind to lie with
her, and she would not let me.

HEARTFREE

Why did not you ravish her?

SIR JOHN

Yes! and so have hedged myself into forty quarrels with her
relations, besides buying my pardon. But, more than all   260
that, you must know I was afraid of being damned in those
days; for I kept sneaking cowardly company, fellows that
went to church, said grace to their meat, and had not the
least tincture of quality about 'em.

HEARTFREE

But I think you are got into a better gang now.   265

SIR JOHN

Zoons, sir, my Lord Rake and I are hand and glove; I
believe we may get our bones broke together tonight.—
Have you a mind to share a frolic?

CONSTANT

Not I, truly; my talent lies to softer exercises.

SIR JOHN

What, a down bed and a strumpet? A pox of venery, I say!—   270
Will you come and drink with me this afternoon?

CONSTANT

I can't drink today, but we'll come and sit an hour with you,
if you will.

SIR JOHN

Phugh, pox, sit an hour! Why can't you drink?

CONSTANT

Because I'm to see my mistress.   275

SIR JOHN

Who's that?

258 *not you* Q1–2 (you not Q3, P)
265 *are* Q1–3 (have P)

CONSTANT
   Why, do you use to tell?
SIR JOHN
   Yes.
CONSTANT
   So won't I.
SIR JOHN
   Why?   280
CONSTANT
   Because 'tis a secret.
SIR JOHN
   Would my wife knew it; 'twould be no secret long.
CONSTANT
   Why, do you think she can't keep a secret?
SIR JOHN
   No more than she can keep Lent.
HEARTFREE
   Prithee, tell it her to try, Constant.   285
SIR JOHN
   No, prithee don't, that I mayn't be plagued with it.
CONSTANT
   I'll hold you a guinea you don't make her tell it you.
SIR JOHN
   I'll hold you a guinea I do.
CONSTANT
   Which way?
SIR JOHN
   Why, I'll beg her not to tell it me.   290
HEARTFREE
   Nay, if anything does it, that will.
CONSTANT
   But do you think, sir—
SIR JOHN
   Oons, sir, I think a woman and a secret are the two im-
   pertinentest themes in the universe! Therefore pray let's
   hear no more of my wife nor your mistress. Damn 'em both   295
   with all my heart, and everything else that daggles a petti-
   coat, except four generous whores, with Betty Sands at the
   head of 'em, who were drunk with my Lord Rake and I ten
   times in a fortnight.   (*Exit* SIR JOHN)

---

296 *daggles* trails through the mud

297 *Betty Sands* a fashionable prostitute who later sold oranges at Drury
     Lane and died in penury in 1699

CONSTANT

Here's a dainty fellow for you! and the veriest coward too.   300
But his usage of his wife makes me ready to stab the villain.

HEARTFREE

Lovers are short-sighted: all their senses run into that of
feeling. This proceeding of his is the only thing on earth
can make your fortune. If anything can prevail with her to
accept of a gallant, 'tis his ill usage of her; for women will do   305
more for revenge than they'll do for the gospel. Prithee,
take heart, I have great hopes for you; and since I can't
bring you quite off of her, I'll endeavour to bring you quite
on; for a whining lover is the damnedest companion upon
earth.   310

CONSTANT

My dear friend, flatter me a little more with these hopes;
for whilst they prevail I have heaven within me, and could
melt with joy.

HEARTFREE

Pray, no melting yet: let things go farther first. This afternoon, perhaps, we shall make some advance. In the mean-   315
while, let's go dine at Locket's, and let hope get you a
stomach.   (*Exeunt*)

Act II, Scene ii

LADY FANCYFULL's *House*
Enter LADY FANCYFULL *and* MADAMOISELLE

LADY FANCYFULL

Did you ever see anything so importune, Madamoiselle?

MADAMOISELLE

Inteed, matam, to say de trute, he want leetel good breeding.

LADY FANCYFULL

Good breeding? He wants to be caned, Madamoiselle. An
insolent fellow!—And yet let me expose my weakness: 'tis
the only man on earth I could resolve to dispense my favours   5
on, were he but a fine gentleman. Well; did men but know

308 *bring you . . . off of* rescue you from
308–9 *bring you . . . on* advance your cause
  1 *importune* vexatious
  2 *want* Q1 (wanted Q2–3, P)

---

316 *Locket's* an expensive tavern near Charing Cross, patronized by Lord
Foppington in *The Relapse* (II.i.229)

how deep an impression a fine gentleman makes in a lady's
heart, they would reduce all their studies to that of good
breeding alone.

Enter CORNET

CORNET
Madam, here's Mr Treble. He has brought home the verses   10
your ladyship made, and gave him to set.
LADY FANCYFULL
Oh, let him come in by all means. [*Exit* CORNET]—Now,
Madamoiselle, am I going to be unspeakably happy.

Enter TREBLE [*and* PIPE]

So, Mr Treble, you have set my little dialogue?
TREBLE
Yes, madam, and I hope your ladyship will be pleased with   15
it.
LADY FANCYFULL
Oh, no doubt on't; for really, Mr Treble, you set all things
to a wonder. But your music is in particular heavenly when
you have my words to clothe in't.
TREBLE
Your words themselves, madam, have so much music in   20
'em, they inspire me.
LADY FANCYFULL
Nay, now you make me blush, Mr Treble; but pray let's
hear what you have done.
TREBLE
You shall, madam.

A SONG TO BE SUNG BETWEEN A MAN AND A WOMAN
[TREBLE] MAN   Ah, lovely nymph, the world's on fire;   25
                  Veil, veil those cruel eyes.
[PIPE]   WOMAN The world may then in flames expire,
                  And boast that so it dies.
[TREBLE] MAN   But when all mortals are destroyed,
                  Who then shall sing your praise?   30
[PIPE]   WOMAN Those who are fit to be employed:
                  The gods shall altars raise.

---

13 s.d. [*and* PIPE] Q1 gives Pipe no entry, though she is addressed at 51; if
she comes on with Treble she can rescue him from singing the duet with
himself.

TREBLE

How does your ladyship like it, madam?

LADY FANCYFULL

Rapture! Rapture, Mr Treble! I'm all rapture! O wit and art, what power you have when joined! I must needs tell 35 you the birth of this little dialogue, Mr Treble. Its father was a dream, and its mother was the moon. I dreamt that by an unanimous vote I was chosen queen of that pale world; and that the first time I appeared upon my throne—all my subjects fell in love with me. Just then I waked, and seeing 40 pen, ink and paper lie idle upon the table, I slid into my morning-gown, and writ this impromptu.

TREBLE

So I guess the dialogue, madam, is supposed to be between your majesty and your first minister of state.

LADY FANCYFULL

Just. He as minister advises me to trouble my head about 45 the welfare of my subjects; which I as sovereign find a very impertinent proposal. But is the town so dull, Mr Treble, it affords us never another new song?

TREBLE

Madam, I have one in my pocket, came out but yesterday, if your ladyship pleases to let Mrs Pipe sing it. 50

LADY FANCYFULL

By all means.—Here, Pipe, make what music you can of this song, here.

SONG

I

[PIPE]   Not an angel dwells above,
Half so fair as her I love;
    Heaven knows how she'll receive me: 55
If she smiles, I'm blest indeed;
If she frowns, I'm quickly freed;
    Heaven knows, she ne'er can grieve me.

II

None can love her more than I,
Yet she ne'er shall make me die 60
    If my flame can never warm her.
Lasting beauty I'll adore;
I shall never love her more,
    Cruelty will so deform her.

35 *you have* Q1–2 (have you Q3, P)
42 *impromptu* perhaps a noun
50 *Mrs Pipe* Q1 (Mr Pipe Q2–3, P)
60–1 die. If my flame can never warm her; Q1–3, P

R–C

LADY FANCYFULL

Very well.—This is Heartfree's poetry, without question.　65

TREBLE

Won't your ladyship please to sing yourself this morning?

LADY FANCYFULL

O Lord, Mr Treble, my cold is still so barbarous to refuse
me that pleasure. [*Coughs*] He—he—hem.

TREBLE

I'm very sorry for it, madam. Methinks all mankind should
turn physicians for the cure on't.　70

LADY FANCYFULL

Why truly, to give mankind their due, there's few that
know me but have offered their remedy.

TREBLE

They have reason, madam; for I know nobody sings so
near a cherubin as your ladyship.

LADY FANCYFULL

What I do, I owe chiefly to your skill and care, Mr Treble.　75
People do flatter me, indeed, that I have a voice, and a *je ne
sais quoi* in the conduct of it, that will make music of anything. And truly, I begin to believe so, since what happened
t'other night. Would you think it, Mr Treble? Walking
pretty late in the Park (for I often walk late in the Park, Mr　80
Treble), a whim took me to sing 'Chevy Chase', and—would
you believe it?—next morning I had three copies of verses
and six *billets-doux* at my levee upon it.

TREBLE

And without all dispute you deserved as many more, madam.
Are there any further commands for your ladyship's humble　85
servant?

LADY FANCYFULL

Nothing more at this time, Mr Treble. But I shall expect
you here every morning for this month, to sing my little
matter there to me. I'll reward you for your pains.

TREBLE

O Lord, madam—　90

LADY FANCYFULL

Good morrow, sweet Mr Treble.

76–7 *je ne sais quoi* certain something
83 *billets-doux* ed. (billet-doux Q1–3, P) love-letters

79–80 *Walking ... Park* By night St James's Park was given over to
prostitution.
81 *Chevy Chase* the popular old ballad of Douglas and Percy

TREBLE

Your ladyship's most obedient servant.

(*Exit* TREBLE [*with* PIPE])

Enter SERVANT

SERVANT

Will your ladyship please to dine yet?

LADY FANCYFULL

Yes, let 'em serve. (*Exit* SERVANT)—Sure this Heartfree has
bewitched me, Madamoiselle. You can't imagine how oddly   95
he mixed himself in my thoughts during my rapture e'en
now. I vow 'tis a thousand pities he is not more polished;
don't you think so?

MADAMOISELLE

Matam, I tink it so great pity, dat if I was in your ladyship
place, I take him home in my house, I lock him up in my   100
closet, and I never let him go till I teach him everyting dat
fine laty expect from fine gentelman.

LADY FANCYFULL

Why truly, I believe I should soon subdue his brutality; for
without doubt he has a strange *penchant* to grow fond of me,
in spite of his aversion to the sex, else he would ne'er have   105
taken so much pains about me. Lord, how proud would
some poor creatures be of such a conquest! But I, alas, I
don't know how to receive as a favour what I take to be so
infinitely my due. But what shall I do to new-mould him,
Madamoiselle? for till then he's my utter aversion.   110

MADAMOISELLE

Matam, you must laugh at him in all de place dat you meet
him, and turn into de ridicule all he say and all he do.

LADY FANCYFULL

Why truly, satire has been ever of wondrous use to reform
ill manners. Besides, 'tis my particular talent to ridicule
folks. I can be severe, strangely severe, when I will, Mada-   115
moiselle.—Give me the pen and ink—I find myself whimsical—(*Sitting down to write*) I'll write to him.—(*Rising up
again*) Or I'll let it alone, and be severe upon him that way.—
(*Sitting down*) Yet active severity is better than passive.
—(*Rising*) 'Tis as good let alone too, for every lash I give   120
him, perhaps, he'll take for a favour.—(*Sitting*) Yet 'tis a
thousand pities so much satire should be lost.—(*Rising*) But

104 *penchant* inclination
113 *been ever* Q1–2 (ever been Q3, P)
120 *let* Q1–2 (let it Q3, P)

if it should have a wrong effect upon him, 'twould distract
me.—(*Sitting*) Well, I must write though, after all.—
(*Rising*) Or I'll let it alone, which is the same thing.   125
MADAMOISELLE [*Aside*]
    La voilà déterminée!   (*Exeunt*)

Act III, Scene i

Scene opens. SIR JOHN, LADY BRUTE, *and* BELLINDA [*discovered,*] *rising from the table.* [SERVANTS *in attendance*]

SIR JOHN (*To a servant*)
    Here, take away the things; I expect company. But first
    bring me a pipe; I'll smoke.
        [SERVANTS *bring* SIR JOHN *a pipe, &c., clear the table, and
                                                    exeunt*]
LADY BRUTE
    Lord, Sir John, I wonder you won't leave that nasty custom.
SIR JOHN
    Prithee, don't be impertinent.
BELLINDA (*To* LADY BRUTE [*aside*])
    I wonder who those are he expects this afternoon?   5
LADY BRUTE
    I'd give the world to know! Perhaps 'tis Constant; he comes
    here sometimes. If it does prove him, I'm resolved I'll
    share the visit.
BELLINDA
    We'll send for our work and sit here.
LADY BRUTE
    He'll choke us with his tobacco.   10
BELLINDA
    Nothing will choke us when we are doing what we have a
    mind to.—Lovewell!

Enter LOVEWELL

LOVEWELL
    Madam.

126 *La voilà déterminée!* I see she's made up her mind!
126 s.d. (*Exeunt*) Q1 follows this with 'The End of the Second Act'.

---

s.d. *Scene opens* i.e., the two halves of the back-scene are drawn apart
    on shutters to reveal Sir John's dining room
12 *Lovewell!* printed after a long space in Q1. As Zimansky suggests,
    perhaps a speech prefix for Lady Brute was dropped.

LADY BRUTE
Here; bring my cousin's work and mine hither.
             (*Exit* LOVEWELL *and re-enters with their work*)
SIR JOHN
Why, pox, can't you work somewhere else?   15
LADY BRUTE
We shall be careful not to disturb you, sir.
                        [*Exit* LOVEWELL]
BELLINDA
Your pipe would make you too thoughtful, uncle, if you
were left alone; our prittle-prattle will cure your spleen.
SIR JOHN (*Sitting and smoking*)
Will it so, Mrs Pert? Now I believe it will so increase it, I
shall take my own house for a paper-mill.   20
LADY BRUTE (*To* BELLINDA, *aside*)
Don't let's mind him; let him say what he will.
SIR JOHN (*Aside*)
A woman's tongue a cure for the spleen!—Oons! If a man
had got the headache, they'd be for applying the same
remedy.
LADY BRUTE
You have done a great deal, Bellinda, since yesterday.   25
BELLINDA
Yes, I have worked very hard; how do you like it?
LADY BRUTE
Oh, 'tis the prettiest fringe in the world! Well, cousin, you
have the happiest fancy; prithee, advise me about altering
my crimson petticoat.
SIR JOHN
A pox o'your petticoat! Here's such a prating, a man can't   30
digest his own thoughts for you.
LADY BRUTE
(*Aside*) Don't answer him.—[*Aloud*] Well, what do you
advise me?
BELLINDA
Why, really, I would not alter it at all. Methinks 'tis very
pretty as it is.   35
LADY BRUTE
Ay, that's true; but you know one grows weary of the
prettiest things in the world, when one has had 'em long.

15 *Why* ed. (Whu Q1–3, P, perhaps an exclamation)
17 *would* Q1 (will Q2–3, P)

---

20 *paper-mill* i.e., somewhere very noisy; Dobrée cites Etherege, *Love in a
Tub* (I.ii.112): 'Sh'as made more noise then half a dozen Paper-mills'

SIR JOHN
Yes, I have taught her that.

BELLINDA [*To* LADY BRUTE, *aside*]
Shall we provoke him a little?

LADY BRUTE
With all my heart.—[*Aloud*] Bellinda, don't you long to be   40
married?

BELLINDA
Why, there are some things in't I could like well enough.

LADY BRUTE
What do you think you should dislike?

BELLINDA
My husband, a hundred to one else.

LADY BRUTE
Oh, ye wicked wretch! Sure you don't speak as you think?   45

BELLINDA
Yes, I do; especially if he smoked tobacco.
                              (*He looks earnestly at 'em*)

LADY BRUTE
Why, that many times takes off worse smells.

BELLINDA
Then he must smell very ill indeed.

LADY BRUTE
So some men will, to keep their wives from coming near 'em.

BELLINDA
Then those wives should cuckold 'em at a distance.   50

SIR JOHN
Oons, get you gone upstairs, you confederating strumpets
you, or I'll cuckold you with a vengeance!

*He rises in a fury, throws his pipe at 'em, and drives 'em
out. As they run off,* CONSTANT *and* HEARTFREE *enter.* LADY
BRUTE *runs against* CONSTANT

LADY BRUTE
O Lord, he'll beat us, he'll beat us! Dear, dear Mr Constant,
save us!   (*Exeunt* [LADY BRUTE *and* BELLINDA])

SIR JOHN
I'll cuckold you, with a pox!   55

CONSTANT
Heavens, Sir John! What's the matter?

42 *in't* Q1 (in it Q2-3, P)
52 s.d. *He . . . against* CONSTANT Q1 prints this before Sir John's line

SIR JOHN

Sure, if woman had been ready created, the devil, instead
of being kicked down into hell, had been married.

HEARTFREE

Why, what new plague have you found now?

SIR JOHN

Why, these two gentlewomen did but hear me say I expected   60
you here this afternoon; upon which they presently resolved
to take up the room, o'purpose to plague me and my friends.

CONSTANT

Was that all? Why, we should have been glad of their
company.

SIR JOHN

Then I should have been weary of yours, for I can't relish   65
both together. They found fault with my smoking tobacco,
too; and said men stunk. But I have a good mind—to say
something.

CONSTANT

No, nothing against the ladies, pray.

SIR JOHN

Split the ladies! Come, will you sit down?—[*Calling a*   70
SERVANT] Give us some wine, fellow.—You won't smoke?

CONSTANT

No, nor drink neither, at this time; I must ask your pardon.

SIR JOHN

What, this mistress of yours runs in your head! I'll warrant
it's some such squeamish minx as my wife, that's grown so
dainty of late she finds fault even with a dirty shirt.   75

HEARTFREE

That a woman may do, and not be very dainty neither.

SIR JOHN

Pox o'the women! let's drink. Come, you shall take one glass,
though I send for a box of lozenges to sweeten your mouth
after it.

CONSTANT

Nay, if one glass will satisfy you, I'll drink it without putting   80
you to that expense.

SIR JOHN

Why, that's honest.—Fill some wine, sirrah! So.—Here's
to you, gentlemen!—A wife's the devil. To your being both
married!

HEARTFREE

Oh, your most humble servant, sir!   (*They drink*)   85

57 *woman* Q1–2 (women Q3, P)
85 s.d. (*They drink*) Q1 prints this before Heartfree's line

SIR JOHN
Well, how do you like my wine?

CONSTANT
'Tis very good indeed.

HEARTFREE
'Tis admirable.

SIR JOHN
Then give us t'other glass.

CONSTANT
No, pray excuse us now. We'll come another time, and then   90
we won't spare it.

SIR JOHN
This one glass, and no more. Come, it shall be your mistress's health—and that's a great compliment from me, I
assure you.

CONSTANT
And 'tis a very obliging one to me; so give us the glasses.   95

SIR JOHN
So. Let her live—

HEARTFREE
And be kind!   ([*They drink.*] SIR JOHN *coughs in the glass*)

CONSTANT
What's the matter? Does't go the wrong way?

SIR JOHN
If I had love enough to be jealous, I should take this for an
ill omen; for I never drank my wife's health in my life, but   100
I puked in the glass.

CONSTANT
Oh, she's too virtuous to make a reasonable man jealous.

SIR JOHN
Pox of her virtue! If I could but catch her adulterating, I
might be divorced from her by law.

HEARTFREE
And so pay her a yearly pension, to be a distinguished   105
cuckold.

Enter SERVANT

[SERVANT]
Sir, there's my Lord Rake, Colonel Bully, and some other
gentlemen at 'The Blue Posts', desire your company. [*Exit*]

98 *Does't* Q1 (Does it Q2–3, P)

103–6 See note to I.i.53–4.
108 'The Blue Posts' a fashionable tavern in the Haymarket, so named from
     the colour of its door jambs; Sir Jolly Jumble dines there in Otway's
     The Soldier's Fortune (I.i.294)

SIR JOHN
Cod's so, we are to consult about playing the devil tonight.
HEARTFREE
Well, we won't hinder business.   110
SIR JOHN
Methinks I don't know how to leave you, though. But for
once I must make bold.—Or look you, maybe the conference
mayn't last long; so if you'll wait here half an hour, or an
hour, if I don't come then—why, then—I won't come at all.
HEARTFREE (*To* CONSTANT, *aside*)
A good modest proposition, truly!   115
CONSTANT
But let's accept on't, however. Who knows what may
happen?
HEARTFREE [*Aloud*]
Well, sir, to show you how fond we are of your company,
we'll expect your return as long as we can.
SIR JOHN
Nay, maybe I mayn't stay at all; but business, you know,   120
must be done. So, your servant.—Or hark you, if you have
a mind to take a frisk with us, I have an interest with my
lord, I can easily introduce you.
CONSTANT
We are much beholding to you, but for my part I'm engaged
another way.   125
SIR JOHN
What? To your mistress, I'll warrant! Prithee leave your
nasty punk to entertain herself with her own lewd thoughts,
and make one with us tonight.
CONSTANT
Sir, 'tis business that is to employ me.
HEARTFREE
And me; and business must be done, you know.   130
SIR JOHN
Ay, women's business, though the world were consumed
for't.   (*Exit* SIR JOHN [*followed by* SERVANT])
CONSTANT
Farewell, beast!—And now, my dear friend, would my

109 *Cod's* a perversion of *God's*
119 *expect* await (also at 292)
124 *beholding* Q1–3 (beholden P)

_____

132 s.d. [*followed by* SERVANT] The servant who poured wine in 82 may have
    been silently dismissed already; this is his last chance to get off stage
    before the lovers' quartet.

mistress be but as complaisant as some men's wives, who
think it a piece of good breeding to receive the visits of their　135
husband's friends in his absence!

HEARTFREE
Why, for your sake I could forgive her, though she should
be so complaisant to receive something else in his absence.
But what way shall we invent to see her?

CONSTANT
Oh, ne'er hope it! Invention will prove as vain as wishes.　140

Enter LADY BRUTE *and* BELLINDA

HEARTFREE [*To* CONSTANT, *aside*]
What do you think now, friend?

CONSTANT
I think I shall swoon.

HEARTFREE
I'll speak first then, whilst you fetch breath.

LADY BRUTE
We think ourselves obliged, gentlemen, to come and return
you thanks for your knight-errantry. We were just upon　145
being devoured by the fiery dragon.

BELLINDA
Did not his fumes almost knock you down, gentlemen?

HEARTFREE
Truly, ladies, we did undergo some hardships, and should
have done more, if some greater heroes than ourselves hard
by had not diverted him.　150

CONSTANT
Though I am glad of the service you are pleased to say we
have done you, yet I'm sorry we could do it no other way
than by making ourselves privy to what you would perhaps
have kept a secret.

LADY BRUTE
For Sir John's part, I suppose he designed it no secret,　155
since he made so much noise. And for myself, truly I am
not much concerned, since 'tis fallen only into this gentleman's hands and yours; who, I have many reasons to
believe, will neither interpret nor report anything to my
disadvantage.　160

CONSTANT
Your good opinion, madam, was what I feared I never
could have merited.

152 *it* Q1–3 (it in P)

LADY BRUTE
Your fears were vain then, sir; for I am just to everybody.
HEARTFREE
Prithee, Constant, what is't you do to get the ladies' good
opinions, for I'm a novice at it?   165
BELLINDA
Sir, will you give me leave to instruct you?
HEARTFREE
Yes, that I will, with all my soul, madam.
BELLINDA
Why then, you must never be slovenly, never be out of
humour, fare well and cry roast meat, smoke tobacco, nor
drink but when you are a-dry.   170
HEARTFREE
That's hard.
CONSTANT
Nay, if you take his bottle from him, you break his heart,
madam.
BELLINDA
Why, is it possible the gentleman can love drinking?
HEARTFREE
Only by way of antidote.   175
BELLINDA
Against what, pray?
HEARTFREE
Against love, madam.
LADY BRUTE
Are you afraid of being in love, sir?
HEARTFREE
I should, if there were any danger of it.
LADY BRUTE
Pray, why so?   180
HEARTFREE
Because I always had an aversion to being used like a dog.
BELLINDA
Why truly, men in love are seldom used better.
LADY BRUTE
But was you never in love, sir?
HEARTFREE
No, I thank heaven, madam.
BELLINDA
Pray, where got you your learning, then?   185

169 *cry roast meat* advertise your good luck

---

182 Does Bellinda agree with Heartfree or contradict him?

HEARTFREE

From other people's expense.

BELLINDA

That's being a sponger, sir, which is scarce honest; if you'd
buy some experience with your own money, as 'twould be
fairlier got, so 'twould stick longer by you.

Enter FOOTMAN

FOOTMAN

Madam, here's my Lady Fancyfull to wait upon your   190
ladyship.   [*Exit*]

LADY BRUTE

Shield me, kind heaven! What an inundation of impertinence is here coming upon us!

Enter LADY FANCYFULL, *who runs first to* LADY BRUTE,
then to BELLINDA, *kissing 'em*

LADY FANCYFULL

My dear Lady Brute! And sweet Bellinda! Methinks 'tis
an age since I saw you.   195

LADY BRUTE

Yet 'tis but three days; sure you have passed your time very
ill, it seems so long to you.

LADY FANCYFULL

Why really, to confess the truth to you, I am so everlastingly
fatigued with the addresses of unfortunate gentlemen, that
were it not for the extravagancy of the example I should   200
e'en tear out these wicked eyes with my own fingers, to
make both myself and mankind easy.—What think you
on't, Mr Heartfree, for I take you to be my faithful adviser?

HEARTFREE

Why truly, madam—I think every project that is for the
good of mankind ought to be encouraged.   205

LADY FANCYFULL

Then I have your consent, sir?

HEARTFREE

To do whatever you please, madam.

LADY FANCYFULL

You had a much more limited complaisance this morning,
sir.—Would you believe it, ladies? The gentleman has been
so exceeding generous, to tell me of above fifty faults in less 210
time than it was well possible for me to commit two of 'em.

CONSTANT

Why truly, madam, my friend there is apt to be something
familiar with the ladies.

LADY FANCYFULL

He is indeed, sir, but he's wondrous charitable with it; he
has had the goodness to design a reformation, even down   215
to my fingers' ends.—'Twas thus, I think, sir, you would
have had 'em stand. (*Opening her fingers in an awkward
manner*)—My eyes, too, he did not like.—How was't you
would have directed 'em? Thus, I think. (*Staring at him*)—
Then there was something amiss in my gait, too; I don't   220
know well how 'twas, but as I take it he would have had me
walk like him.—Pray, sir, do me the favour to take a turn
or two about the room, that the company may see you.—
He's sullen, ladies, and won't. But, to make short, and give
you as true an idea as I can of the matter, I think 'twas   225
much about this figure in general he would have moulded
me to. (*She walks awkwardly about, staring and looking
ungainly, then changes on a sudden to the extremity of her usual
affectation*) But I was an obstinate woman, and could not
resolve to make myself mistress of his heart by growing as   230
awkward as his fancy.

    (*Here* CONSTANT *and* LADY BRUTE *talk together apart*)

HEARTFREE

Just thus women do, when they think we are in love with
'em, or when they are so with us.

LADY FANCYFULL

'Twould, however, be less vanity for me to conclude the
former than you the latter, sir.   235

HEARTFREE

Madam, all I shall presume to conclude is, that if I were in
love, you'd find the means to make me soon weary on't.

LADY FANCYFULL

Not by over-fondness, upon my word, sir. But pray let's
stop here, for you are so much governed by instinct I know
you'll grow brutish at last.   240

BELLINDA

(*Aside*) Now am I sure she's fond of him. I'll try to make
her jealous.—[*Aloud*] Well, for my part, I should be glad
to find somebody would be so free with me, that I might
know my faults and mend 'em.

LADY FANCYFULL

Then pray let me recommend this gentleman to you: I have   245
known him some time and will be surety for him, that upon
a very limited encouragement on your side, you shall find an
extended impudence on his.

216 *you would* Q1–2 (you'ld Q3, you'd P)
241 *am I* Q1 (I am Q2–3, I'm P)

HEARTFREE

I thank you, madam, for your recommendation; but, hating
idleness, I'm unwilling to enter into a place where I believe　250
there would be nothing to do. I was fond of serving your
ladyship, because I knew you'd find me constant employ-
ment.

LADY FANCYFULL

I told you he'd be rude, Bellinda.

BELLINDA

Oh, a little bluntness is a sign of honesty, which makes me　255
always ready to pardon it.—So, sir, if you have no other
exceptions to my service but the fear of being idle in't, you
may venture to 'list yourself; I shall find you work, I warrant
you.

HEARTFREE

Upon those terms I engage, madam; and this (with your　260
leave) I take for earnest.　　　　　(*Offering to kiss her hand*)

BELLINDA

Hold there, sir! I'm none of your earnest-givers. But if I'm
well served, I give good wages and pay punctually.

　　　　　(HEARTFREE *and* BELLINDA *seem to continue talking*
　　　　　　　　　　　　　　　　　　　　　　familiarly)

LADY FANCYFULL

(*Aside*) I don't like this jesting between 'em. Methinks the
fool begins to look as if he were in earnest—but then he　265
must be a fool indeed.—(*Looking at* BELLINDA *scornfully*)
Lard, what a difference there is between me and her! How
I should despise such a thing, if I were a man! What a nose
she has! What a chin! What a neck!—Then her eyes!—
And the worst kissing lips in the universe!—No, no, he can　270
never like her, that's positive.—Yet I can't suffer 'em
together any longer.—[*Aloud*] Mr Heartfree! Do you know
that you and I must have no quarrel for all this? I can't
forbear being a little severe now and then; but women, you
know, may be allowed anything.　　　　　　　　　　　275

HEARTFREE

Up to a certain age, madam.

LADY FANCYFULL

Which I am not yet past, I hope.

261 *for earnest* (1) in all seriousness (2) as a downpayment to secure the
contract (3) as a foretaste of what is to come

HEARTFREE (*Aside*)

Nor never will, I dare swear.

LADY FANCYFULL (*To* LADY BRUTE)

Come, madam; will your ladyship be witness to our recon-
ciliation?   280

LADY BRUTE

You agree, then, at last?

HEARTFREE (*Slightingly*)

We forgive.

LADY FANCYFULL (*Aside*)

That was a cold ill-natured reply.

LADY BRUTE

Then there's no challenges sent between you?

HEARTFREE

Not from me, I promise.—(*Aside, to* CONSTANT) But that's   285
more than I'll do for her, for I know she can as well be
damned as forbear writing to me.

CONSTANT

That I believe. But I think we had best be going, lest she
should suspect something and be malicious.

HEARTFREE

With all my heart.   290

CONSTANT [*Aloud*]

Ladies, we are your humble servants. I see Sir John is quite
engaged; 'twould be in vain to expect him.—Come, Heartfree.   (*Exit*)

HEARTFREE

Ladies, your servant.—(*To* BELLINDA) I hope, madam, you
won't forget our bargain; I'm to say what I please to you.   295

BELLINDA

Liberty of speech entire, sir.   (*Exit* HEARTFREE)

LADY FANCYFULL

(*Aside*) Very pretty, truly.—But how the blockhead went
out! languishing at her, and not a look toward me! Well;
churchmen may talk, but miracles are not ceased. For 'tis
more than natural such a rude fellow as he, and such a little   300
impertinent as she, should be capable of making a woman
of my sphere uneasy. But I can bear her sight no longer;
methinks she's grown ten times uglier than Cornet. I must
go home, and study revenge.—(*To* LADY BRUTE) Madam,
your humble servant; I must take my leave.   305

---

296 s.d. (*Exit* HEARTFREE) Q1 prints this before Bellinda's line
304 *go home* Q1–2 (home Q3, P)

LADY BRUTE
> What, going already, madam?

LADY FANCYFULL
> I must beg you'll excuse me this once, for really I have
> eighteen visits to return this afternoon; so you see I'm
> importuned by the women as well as the men.

BELLINDA (*Aside*)
> And she's quits with 'em both.   310

LADY FANCYFULL (*Going*)
> Nay, you shan't go one step out of the room.

LADY BRUTE
> Indeed, I'll wait upon you down.

LADY FANCYFULL
> No, sweet Lady Brute; you know I swoon at ceremony.

LADY BRUTE
> Pray, give me leave.

LADY FANCYFULL
> You know I won't.   315

LADY BRUTE
> Indeed I must.

LADY FANCYFULL
> Indeed you shan't.

LADY BRUTE
> Indeed I will.

LADY FANCYFULL
> Indeed you shan't.

LADY BRUTE
> Indeed I will.   320

LADY FANCYFULL
> Indeed you shan't. Indeed, indeed, indeed you shan't!
>> (*Exit* LADY FANCYFULL *running.* [LADY BRUTE *and*
>>   BELLINDA] *follow*)

Re-enter LADY BRUTE, *sola*

[LADY BRUTE]
> This impertinent woman has put me out of humour for a
> fortnight.—What an agreeable moment has her foolish visit
> interrupted! Lord, how like a torrent love flows into the

310 *she's* Q1, P (she Q2–3)
310 *'em* Q1–2 (them Q3, P)
321 s.d. LADY BRUTE *and* BELLINDA ed. (*They* Q1)

---

311 s.p. LADY FANCYFULL (*Going*) Q1 prints this as a stage direction, thus
    making 311 a continuation of Bellinda's speech; but she has no reason
    to prevent Lady Fancyfull's departure.

heart when once the sluice of desire is opened! Good gods!   325
What a pleasure there is in doing what we should not do!

Re-enter CONSTANT

Ha! Here again?

CONSTANT

Though the renewing my visit may seem a little irregular,
I hope I shall obtain your pardon for it, madam, when you
know I only left the room lest the lady who was here should   330
have been as malicious in her remarks as she's foolish in her
conduct.

LADY BRUTE

He who has discretion enough to be tender of a woman's
reputation carries a virtue about him may atone for a great
many faults.   335

CONSTANT

If it has a title to atone for any, its pretensions must needs
be strongest where the crime is love. I therefore hope I shall
be forgiven the attempt I have made upon your heart, since
my enterprise has been a secret to all the world but yourself.

LADY BRUTE

Secrecy indeed in sins of this kind is an argument of weight   340
to lessen the punishment; but nothing's a plea for a pardon
entire, without a sincere repentance.

CONSTANT

If sincerity in repentance consist in sorrow for offending, no
cloister ever enclosed so true a penitent as I should be. But I
hope it cannot be reckoned an offence to love, where 'tis a   345
duty to adore.

LADY BRUTE

'Tis an offence, a great one, where it would rob a woman of
all she ought to be adored for—her virtue.

CONSTANT

Virtue?—Virtue, alas, is no more like the thing that's called
so, than 'tis like vice itself. Virtue consists in goodness,   350
honour, gratitude, sincerity and pity; and not in peevish,
snarling, strait-laced chastity. True virtue, wheresoe'er it
moves, still carries an intrinsic worth about it, and is in
every place and in each sex of equal value. So is not continence, you see—that phantom of honour, which men in   355

336 *title* claim
343 *consist* Q1–2 (consists Q3, P)
354–5 *continence* (1) marital chastity (2) virgin abstinence

every age have so condemned they have thrown it amongst
the women to scrabble for.

LADY BRUTE

If it be a thing of so very little value, why do you so earnestly
recommend it to your wives and daughters?

CONSTANT

We recommend it to our wives, madam, because we would   360
keep 'em to ourselves; and to our daughters, because we
would dispose of 'em to others.

LADY BRUTE

'Tis then of some importance, it seems, since you can't
dispose of 'em without it.

CONSTANT

That importance, madam, lies in the humour of the country,   365
not in the nature of the thing.

LADY BRUTE

How do you prove that, sir?

CONSTANT

From the wisdom of a neighbouring nation in a contrary
practice. In monarchies things go by whimsy, but common-
wealths weigh all things in the scale of reason.   370

LADY BRUTE

I hope we are not so very light a people to bring up fashions
without some ground.

CONSTANT

Pray what does your ladyship think of a powdered coat for
deep mourning?

LADY BRUTE

I think, sir, your sophistry has all the effect that you can   375
reasonably expect it should have; it puzzles, but don't
convince.

CONSTANT

I'm sorry for it.

LADY BRUTE

I'm sorry to hear you say so.

CONSTANT

Pray why?   380

LADY BRUTE

Because if you expected more from it, you have a worse
opinion of my understanding than I desire you should have.

357 *scrabble for* struggle or scramble for
364 *'em* Q1–3 (them P)
371 *bring up* introduce and popularize
373 *powdered* minutely decorated

CONSTANT

(*Aside*) I comprehend her: she would have me set a value
upon her chastity, that I may think myself the more obliged
to her when she makes me a present of it.—(*To her*) I beg   385
you will believe I did but rally, madam; I know you judge
too well of right and wrong to be deceived by arguments
like those. I hope you'll have so favourable an opinion of
my understanding, too, to believe the thing called virtue
has worth enough with me to pass for an eternal obligation   390
where'er 'tis sacrificed.

LADY BRUTE

It is, I think, so great a one as nothing can repay.

CONSTANT

Yes; the making the man you love your everlasting debtor.

LADY BRUTE

When debtors once have borrowed all we have to lend, they
are very apt to grow shy of their creditors' company.   395

CONSTANT

That, madam, is only when they are forced to borrow of
usurers, and not of a generous friend. Let us choose our
creditors, and we are seldom so ungrateful to shun 'em.

LADY BRUTE

What think you of Sir John, sir? I was his free choice.

CONSTANT

I think he's married, madam.   400

LADY BRUTE

Does marriage then exclude men from your rule of constancy?

CONSTANT

It does. Constancy's a brave, free, haughty, generous agent,
that cannot buckle to the chains of wedlock. There's a poor
sordid slavery in marriage, that turns the flowing tide of   405
honour and sinks us to the lowest ebb of infamy. 'Tis a
corrupted soil; ill nature, avarice, sloth, cowardice and dirt
are all its product.

LADY BRUTE

Have you no exceptions to this general rule, as well as to
t'other?   410

CONSTANT

Yes; I would (after all) be an exception to it myself, if you
were free in power and will to make me so.

384 *may* Q1–3 (might P)
395 *shy* P (very shy Q1–3, perhaps repeated from *very apt*)
404 *buckle* submit

LADY BRUTE

Compliments are well placed, where 'tis impossible to lay hold on 'em.

CONSTANT

I would to heaven 'twere possible for you to lay hold on   415
mine, that you might see it is no compliment at all. But since you are already disposed on, beyond redemption, to one who does not know the value of the jewel you have put into his hands, I hope you would not think him greatly wronged though it should sometimes be looked on by a   420
friend, who knows how to esteem it as he ought.

LADY BRUTE

If looking on't alone would serve his turn, the wrong perhaps might not be very great.

CONSTANT

Why, what if he should wear it now and then a day, so he gave good security to bring it home again at night?   425

LADY BRUTE

Small security, I fancy, might serve for that. One might venture to take his word.

CONSTANT

Then where's the injury to the owner?

LADY BRUTE

'Tis an injury to him if he think it one. For if happiness be seated in the mind, unhappiness must be so too.   430

CONSTANT

Here I close with you, madam, and draw my conclusive argument from your own position: if the injury lie in the fancy, there needs nothing but secrecy to prevent the wrong.

LADY BRUTE (*Going*)

A surer way to prevent it, is to hear no more arguments in its behalf.   435

CONSTANT (*Following her*)

But, madam—

LADY BRUTE

But, sir, 'tis my turn to be discreet now, and not suffer too long a visit.

CONSTANT (*Catching her hand*)

By heaven, you shall not stir, till you give me hopes that I shall see you again at some more convenient time and place.   440

LADY BRUTE

I give you just hopes enough—(*Breaking from him*) to get

417 *disposed on* Q1–3 (disposed of P)
429 *an injury* Q1–2 (injury Q3, P)

loose from you; and that's all I can afford you at this time.

(Exit running)

CONSTANT *(Solus)*

Now, by all that's great and good, she is a charming woman!
In what ecstasy of joy she has left me! For she gave me hope;
did she not say she gave me hope?—Hope? Ay. What hope?   445
—Enough to make me let her go! Why, that's enough in
conscience. Or no matter how 'twas spoke; hope was the
word: it came from her and it was said to me.

Enter HEARTFREE

Ha, Heartfree! Thou hast done me noble service in prattling
to the young gentlewoman without there; come to my arms,   450
thou venerable bawd, and let me squeeze thee (*Embracing
him eagerly*) as a new pair of stays does a fat country girl,
when she's carried to court to stand for a maid of honour.

HEARTFREE

Why, what the devil's all this rapture for?

CONSTANT

Rapture? There's ground for rapture, man; there's hopes,   455
my Heartfree; hopes, my friend!

HEARTFREE

Hopes! of what?

CONSTANT

Why, hopes that my lady and I together (for 'tis more than
one body's work) should make Sir John a cuckold.

HEARTFREE

Prithee, what did she say to thee?   460

CONSTANT

Say? What did she not say! She said that—says she—she
said—Zoons, I don't know what she said, but she looked as
if she said everything I'd have her; and so if thou'lt go to
the tavern, I'll treat thee with anything that gold can buy;
I'll give all my silver amongst the drawers, make a bonfire   465
before the door, say the plenipos have signed the peace,
and the Bank of England's grown honest.   *(Exeunt)*

465–6 *make ... peace* Negotiations to end the Continental War had begun
in May 1696; plenipotentiaries left England in March 1697, and the
Treaty of Ryswick was signed on 10 September; when Matthew Prior
brought the news to London on 14 September, bonfires were lit in the
streets. (All dates are Old Style.)

467 *Bank of England* founded in 1694, badly shaken by the currency crisis
of 1696, and not yet beyond charges of corruption

Act III, Scene ii

Scene opens. LORD RAKE, SIR JOHN, [COLONEL BULLY] &c.
[*discovered*] *at a table, drinking*

ALL
  Huzza!
LORD RAKE
  Come, boys, charge again.—So.—Confusion to all order!
  Here's liberty of conscience!
ALL
  Huzza!
LORD RAKE
  I'll sing you a song I made this morning to this purpose.   5
SIR JOHN
  'Tis wicked, I hope.
COLONEL BULLY
  Don't my lord tell you he made it?
SIR JOHN
  Well then, let's ha't.
LORD RAKE (*Sings*)

I

What a pother of late
Have they kept in the state   10
  About setting our consciences free!
A bottle has more
Dispensation in store,
  Than the king and the state can decree.

II

When my head's full of wine,   15
I o'erflow with design,
  And know no penal laws that can curb me.

---

s.d. *Scene opens* as in III.i, to reveal a room in 'The Blue Posts'. As the
text stands, there has been no opportunity to strike the furniture used
in III.i. One solution would be an act-interval before III.ii; another,
to play the end of III.i against a back-scene set well down-stage.
Garrick's promptbook moves the action to Lady Brute's chamber, set
in the first grooves, at III.i.321.

3 *liberty of conscience* granted to dissenters by the Toleration Act of 1689
and the Quaker Act of 1696

13 *Dispensation* the king's power to suspend the law in an individual case,
invoked by James II to give Roman Catholics military office

17 *penal laws* rarely enforced against Roman Catholics in England, but
applied in Ireland after 1695 with great severity

Whate'er I devise
Seems good in my eyes,
    And religion ne'er dares to disturb me.   20
                        III
No saucy remorse
Intrudes in my course,
    Nor impertinent notions of evil;
So there's claret in store,
In peace I've my whore,   25
    And in peace I jog on to the devil.
ALL (*Sing*) So there's claret, &c.
LORD RAKE (*Repeats*)
    And in peace I jog on to the devil.

Well, how do you like it, gentlemen?
ALL
Oh, admirable!   30
SIR JOHN
I would not give a fig for a song that is not full of sin and
impudence.
LORD RAKE
Then my muse is to your taste. But drink away; the night
steals upon us; we shall want time to be lewd in.—Hey,
page!   35

                    [*Enter* PAGE]

Sally out, sirrah, and see what's doing in the camp; we'll
beat up their quarters presently.
PAGE
I'll bring your lordship an exact account.   (*Exit* PAGE)
LORD RAKE
Now let the spirit of clary go round! Fill me a brimmer.
Here's to our forlorn hope! Courage, knight; victory attends 40
you!
SIR JOHN
And laurels shall crown me. Drink away and be damned!
LORD RAKE
Again, boys; t'other glass, and damn morality!
SIR JOHN (*Drunk*)
Ay—damn morality—and damn the watch! And let the
constable be married!   45

40 *forlorn hope* storming party

---

37 *beat ... quarters* visit their lodgings unexpectedly; a military phrase
    used here for a night raid on a bawdy house
39 *clary* brandy flavoured with honey, spices, and clary-flowers

ALL
    Huzza!

Re-enter PAGE

LORD RAKE
    How are the streets inhabited, sirrah?
PAGE
    My lord, it's Sunday night; they are full of drunken
    citizens.   [*Exit*]
LORD RAKE
    Along then, boys; we shall have a feast.   50
COLONEL BULLY
    Along, noble knight.
SIR JOHN
    Ay—along, Bully; and he that says Sir John Brute is not as
    drunk and as religious as the drunkenest citizen of 'em all—
    is a liar, and the son of a whore.
COLONEL BULLY
    Why, that was bravely spoke, and like a free-born English-   55
    man.
SIR JOHN
    What's that to you, sir, whether I am an Englishman or a
    Frenchman?
COLONEL BULLY
    Zoons, you are not angry, sir?
SIR JOHN
    Zoons, I am angry, sir!—for if I am a free-born Englishman,   60
    what have you to do even to talk of my privileges?
LORD RAKE
    Why prithee, knight, don't quarrel here; leave private
    animosities to be decided by daylight, let the night be
    employed against the public enemy.
SIR JOHN
    My lord, I respect you because you are a man of quality.   65
    But I'll make that fellow know, I am within a hair's breadth
    as absolute by my privileges as the King of France is by his
    prerogative. He by his prerogative takes money where it is
    not his due; I by my privilege refuse paying it where I owe
    it. Liberty and property and Old England, huzza!   70
ALL
    Huzza!   (*Exit* SIR JOHN *reeling, all following him*)

60 *I am a* Q1–2 (I'm a Q3, P)

---

61 *privileges* here, the constitutional rights of a free-born Englishman
68 *prerogative* here, the unrestricted power of an absolute king

Act III, Scene iii

A bedchamber
Enter LADY BRUTE *and* BELLINDA

LADY BRUTE
Sure, it's late, Bellinda; I begin to be sleepy.
BELLINDA
Yes, 'tis near twelve. Will you go to bed?
LADY BRUTE
To bed, my dear? And by that time I'm fallen into a sweet
sleep (or perhaps a sweet dream, which is better and better),
Sir John will come home roaring drunk, and be overjoyed   5
he finds me in a condition to be disturbed.
BELLINDA
Oh, you need not fear him, he's in for all night. The servants
say he's gone to drink with my Lord Rake.
LADY BRUTE
Nay, 'tis not very likely, indeed, such suitable company
should part presently. What hogs men turn, Bellinda, when   10
they grow weary of women!
BELLINDA
And what owls they are whilst they are fond of 'em!
LADY BRUTE
But that we may forgive well enough, because they are so
upon our accounts.
BELLINDA
We ought to do so, indeed; but 'tis a hard matter. For when   15
a man is really in love, he looks so unsufferably silly that
though a woman liked him well enough before, she has then
much ado to endure the sight of him. And this I take to be
the reason why lovers are so generally ill-used.
LADY BRUTE
Well, I own now, I'm well enough pleased to see a man look   20
like an ass for me.
BELLINDA
Ay, I'm pleased he should look like an ass too—that is, I'm
pleased with myself for making him look so.
LADY BRUTE
Nay truly, I think if he'd find some other way to express his
passion, 'twould be more to his advantage.   25

3 *I'm* Q1–3 (I am P)

BELLINDA

Yes; for then a woman might like his passion and him too.

LADY BRUTE

Yet, Bellinda, after all, a woman's life would be but a dull
business if 'twere not for men—and men that can look like
asses, too. We should never blame fate for the shortness of
our days; our time would hang wretchedly upon our hands.   30

BELLINDA

Why truly, they do help us off with a good share on't. For
were there no men in the world, o'my conscience I should
be no longer a-dressing than I'm a-saying my prayers; nay,
though it were Sunday: for you know that one may go to
church without stays on.   35

LADY BRUTE

But don't you think emulation might do something? For
every woman you see desires to be finer than her neighbour.

BELLINDA

That's only that the men may like her better than her neighbour. No; if there were no men, adieu fine petticoats, we
should be weary of wearing 'em.   40

LADY BRUTE

And adieu plays, we should be weary of seeing 'em.

BELLINDA

Adieu Hyde Park, the dust would choke us.

LADY BRUTE

Adieu St James's, walking would tire us.

BELLINDA

Adieu London, the smoke would stifle us.

LADY BRUTE

And adieu going to church, for religion would ne'er prevail   45
with us.

BOTH

Ha ha ha ha ha!

BELLINDA

Our confession is so very hearty, sure we merit absolution.

LADY BRUTE

Not unless we go through with't, and confess all. So prithee,
for the ease of our consciences, let's hide nothing.   50

BELLINDA

Agreed.

34 *know that* Q1–3 (know P)

---

42 *Hyde Park* 'Here People Coach it to take the Air, amidst a Cloud of
   Dust, able to Choak a Foot Soldier' (Tom Brown, *Amusements* (1700),
   p. 55).

LADY BRUTE
Why then, I confess that I love to sit in the forefront of a
box; for if one sits behind, there's two acts gone perhaps before one's found out. And when I am there, if I perceive
the men whispering and looking upon me, you must know   55
I cannot for my life forbear thinking they talk to my advantage; and that sets a thousand little tickling vanities on foot—

BELLINDA
Just my case for all the world; but go on.

LADY BRUTE
I watch with impatience for the next jest in the play, that
I may laugh and show my white teeth. If the poet has been   60
dull and the jest be long a-coming, I pretend to whisper one
to my friend, and from thence fall into a little short discourse
in which I take occasion to show my face in all humours:
brisk, pleased, serious, melancholy, languishing.—Not that
what we say to one another causes any of these alterations,   65
but—

BELLINDA
Don't trouble yourself to explain; for if I'm not mistaken,
you and I have had some of these necessary dialogues before
now, with the same intention.

LADY BRUTE
Why, I'll swear, Bellinda, some people do give strange   70
agreeable airs to their faces in speaking. Tell me true—did
you never practise in the glass?

BELLINDA
Why, did you?

LADY BRUTE
Yes, faith, many a time.

BELLINDA
And I too, I own it; both how to speak myself, and how to   75
look when others speak. But my glass and I could never yet
agree what face I should make when they come blurt out
with a nasty thing in a play. For all the men presently look
upon the women, that's certain; so laugh we must not,
though our stays burst for't, because that's telling truth and   80
owning we understand the jest; and to look serious is so
dull, when the whole house is a-laughing—

60 *may* Q1–3 (might P)
60 *poet* author
62 *short* Q1 (small Q2–3, P)
77 *blurt* blurting (adv.)
78 *nasty* obscene
78 *presently* immediately

LADY BRUTE

Besides, that looking serious does really betray our knowledge in the matter as much as laughing with the company
would do; for if we did not understand the thing, we should   85
naturally do like other people.

BELLINDA

For my part, I always take that occasion to blow my nose.

LADY BRUTE

You must blow your nose half off then at some plays.

BELLINDA

Why don't some reformer or other beat the poet for't?

LADY BRUTE

Because he is not so sure of our private approbation as of   90
our public thanks. Well, sure, there is not upon earth so
impertinent a thing as women's modesty.

BELLINDA

Yes; men's fantasque, that obliges us to it. If we quit our
modesty, they say we lose our charms; and yet they know
that very modesty is affectation, and rail at our hypocrisy.   95

LADY BRUTE

Thus one would think 'twere a hard matter to please 'em,
niece; yet our kind Mother Nature has given us something
that makes amends for all. Let our weakness be what it will,
mankind will still be weaker; and whilst there is a world, 'tis
woman that will govern it. But prithee, one word of poor   100
Constant before we go to bed, if it be but to furnish matter
for dreams; I dare swear he's talking of me now, or thinking
of me at least, though it be in the middle of his prayers.

BELLINDA

So he ought, I think; for you were pleased to make him a
good round advance today, madam.   105

LADY BRUTE

Why, I have e'en plagued him enough to satisfy any reasonable woman. He has besieged me these two years to no
purpose.

BELLINDA

And if he besieged you two years more, he'd be well enough
paid, so he had the plundering of you at last.   110

---

93 *fantasque* fancy, whim

---

89 Bellinda has not read Blackmore's Preface to *Prince Arthur* (1695) or
James Wright's *Country Conversations* (1694), which argues that 'most
of our New Comedies are become the very Pictures of Immorality'
(p. 4).

LADY BRUTE

That may be; but I'm afraid the town won't be able to hold
out much longer: for to confess the truth to you, Bellinda,
the garrison begins to grow mutinous.

BELLINDA

Then the sooner you capitulate, the better.

LADY BRUTE

Yet, methinks, I would fain stay a little longer, to see you   115
fixed too, that we might start together and see who could
love longest. What think you, if Heartfree should have a
month's mind to you?

BELLINDA

Why, faith, I could almost be in love with him for despising
that foolish affected Lady Fancyfull; but I'm afraid he's   120
too cold ever to warm himself by my fire.

LADY BRUTE

Then he deserves to be froze to death. Would I were a man
for your sake, my dear rogue.   (*Kissing her*)

BELLINDA

You'd wish yourself a woman again for your own, or the
men are mistaken. But if I could make a conquest of this son   125
of Bacchus, and rival his bottle, what should I do with him?
He has no fortune; I can't marry him; and sure you would
not have me commit fornication.

LADY BRUTE

Why, if you did, child, 'twould be but a good friendly part;
if 'twere only to keep me in countenance whilst I commit—   130
you know what.

BELLINDA

Well, if I can't resolve to serve you that way, I may perhaps
some other, as much to your satisfaction. But pray, how
shall we contrive to see these blades again quickly?

LADY BRUTE

We must e'en have recourse to the old way; make 'em an   135
appointment 'twixt jest and earnest. 'Twill look like a frolic,
and that you know's a very good thing to save a woman's
blushes.

BELLINDA

You advise well; but where shall it be?

118 *month's mind* strong inclination
123 *my dear* Q1–3 (dear P)

LADY BRUTE

In Spring Garden. But they shan't know their women till   140
their women pull off their masks; for a surprise is the most
agreeable thing in the world, and I find myself in a very
good humour, ready to do 'em any good turn I can think on.

BELLINDA

Then pray write 'em the necessary billet without farther
delay.   145

LADY BRUTE

Let's go into your chamber, then, and whilst you say your
prayers I'll do it, child.   (*Exeunt*)

Act IV, Scene i

Covent Garden
Enter LORD RAKE, SIR JOHN, [COLONEL BULLY] *&c., with*
swords drawn

LORD RAKE

Is the dog dead?

COLONEL BULLY

No, damn him, I heard him wheeze.

LORD RAKE

How the witch his wife howled!

COLONEL BULLY

Ay, she'll alarm the watch presently.

LORD RAKE

Appear, knight, then; come, you have a good cause to fight   5
for: there's a man murdered.

SIR JOHN

Is there? Then let his ghost be satisfied; for I'll sacrifice a
constable to it presently, and burn his body upon his wooden
chair.

Enter a TAILOR, *with a bundle under his arm*

147 s.d. (*Exeunt*) Q1 follows this with 'The End of the Third Act'.

---

140 *Spring Garden* a pleasure garden in Lambeth laid out with close walks,
   secluded arbours, and an artificial wilderness; the *Spectator* wanted
   'more Nightingales, and fewer Strumpets' (no. 383, 20 May 1712)
   s.d. *Covent Garden* a noble square behind the Strand, bounded by
   Inigo Jones's piazzas, St Paul's Church, and a market for earthenware
   and fruit

  8 *constable* officer of a city ward on oath to 'Arrest all them that make
   Contest, Riot, Debate or Affray ... and lead them to the House or
   Compter of one of the *Sheriffs*' (Thomas Delaune, *Angliae Metropolis*
   (1690), p. 247)

COLONEL BULLY

How now! What have we got here, a thief?   10

TAILOR

No, an't please you; I'm no thief.

LORD RAKE

That we'll see presently.—Here, let the general examine
him.

SIR JOHN

Ay, ay; let me examine him, and I'll lay a hundred pound I
find him guilty in spite of his teeth—for he looks—like a—   15
sneaking rascal.—Come sirrah, without equivocation or
mental reservation, tell me of what opinion you are and
what calling; for by them—I shall guess at your morals.

TAILOR

An't please you, I'm a dissenting journeyman tailor.

SIR JOHN

Then, sirrah, you love lying by your religion and theft by   20
your trade. And so, that your punishment may be suitable to
your crimes, I'll have you first gagged—and then hanged.

TAILOR

Pray, good worthy gentlemen, don't abuse me; indeed I'm
an honest man, and a good workman, though I say it that
should not say it.   25

SIR JOHN

No words, sirrah, but attend your fate.

LORD RAKE

Let me see what's in that bundle.

TAILOR

An't please you, it's the doctor of the parish's gown.

LORD RAKE

The doctor's gown!—Hark you, knight, you won't stick at
abusing the clergy, will you?   30

SIR JOHN

No, I'm drunk, and I'll abuse anything—but my wife; and
her I name—with reverence.

LORD RAKE

Then you shall wear this gown whilst you charge the watch,
that though the blows fall upon you, the scandal may light
upon the church.   35

SIR JOHN

A generous design, by all the gods!—Give it me.
                              (*Takes the gown and puts it on*)

28 *it's* Q1–3 (it is P)

---

12 *general* Lord Rake sustains his series of military metaphors.

TAILOR

O dear gentlemen, I shall be quite undone if you take the gown.

SIR JOHN

Retire, sirrah; and since you carry off your skin—go home, and be happy.   40

TAILOR (*Pausing*)

I think I had e'en as good follow the gentleman's friendly advice. For if I dispute any longer, who knows but the whim may take him to case me? These courtiers are fuller of tricks than they are of money; they'll sooner cut a man's throat than pay his bill.   (*Exit* TAILOR)   45

SIR JOHN

So, how d'ye like my shapes now?

LORD RAKE

This will do to a miracle; he looks like a bishop going to the holy war.—But to your arms, gentlemen; the enemy appears.

Enter CONSTABLE *and* WATCH

WATCHMAN

Stand! Who goes there? Come before the constable.

SIR JOHN

The constable's a rascal—and you are the son of a whore.   50

WATCHMAN

A good civil answer for a parson, truly!

CONSTABLE

Methinks, sir, a man of your coat might set a better example.

SIR JOHN

Sirrah, I'll make you know—there are men of my coat can set as bad examples—as you can do, you dog you!

(SIR JOHN *strikes the* CONSTABLE. *They knock him down, disarm him and seize him.* LORD RAKE *&c. run away*)

CONSTABLE

So, we have secured the parson, however.   55

SIR JOHN

Blood and blood—and blood!

WATCHMAN

Lord have mercy upon us! How the wicked wretch raves of blood! I'll warrant he has been murdering somebody tonight.

SIR JOHN

Sirrah, there's nothing got by murder but a halter. My talent   60
lies towards drunkenness and simony.

43 *case* skin

WATCHMAN
Why, that now was spoke like a man of parts, neighbours;
it's pity he should be so disguised.
SIR JOHN
You lie—I am not disguised; for I am drunk barefaced.
WATCHMAN
Look you there again!—This is a mad parson, Mr Con-   65
stable; I'll lay a pot of ale upon's head, he's a good preacher.
CONSTABLE
Come, sir; out of respect to your calling I shan't put you
into the round-house; but we must secure you in our
drawing-room till morning, that you may do no mischief.
So, come along.   70
SIR JOHN
You may put me where you will, sirrah, now you have
overcome me. But if I can't do mischief, I'll think of mis-
chief—in spite of your teeth, you dog you!   (*Exeunt*)

Act IV, Scene ii

A bedchamber
Enter HEARTFREE, *solus*

[HEARTFREE]
What the plague ails me? Love? No, I thank you for that, my
heart's rock still.—Yet 'tis Bellinda that disturbs me, that's
positive.—Well, what of all that? Must I love her for being
troublesome? At that rate I might love all the women I
meet, egad. But hold!—Though I don't love her for disturb-   5
ing me, yet she may disturb me because I love her. Ay, that
may be, faith! I have dreamt of her, that's certain.—Well,
so I have of my mother; therefore what's that to the purpose?
—Ay, but Bellinda runs in my mind waking.—And so does
many a damned thing that I don't care a farthing for!—   10
Methinks, though, I would fain be talking to her, and yet
I have no business.—Well, am I the first man that has had
a mind to do an impertinent thing?

Enter CONSTANT

64 *I am not* Q1–3 (I'm not P)
5 *egad* (I gad Q1) a softened form of *By God* (also at 69)
13 *impertinent* irrelevant or absurd

---

68 *round-house* an overnight lock-up

R–D

CONSTANT
> How now, Heartfree? What makes you up and dressed so
> soon? I thought none but lovers quarreled with their beds;   15
> I expected to have found you snoring, as I used to do.

HEARTFREE
> Why faith, friend, 'tis the care I have of your affairs that
> makes me so thoughtful; I have been studying all night
> how to bring your matter about with Bellinda.

CONSTANT
> With Bellinda?   20

HEARTFREE
> With my lady, I mean.—And faith, I have mighty hopes
> on't. Sure you must be very well satisfied with her behaviour
> to you yesterday?

CONSTANT
> So well, that nothing but a lover's fears can make me doubt
> of success. But what can this sudden change proceed from?   25

HEARTFREE
> Why, you saw her husband beat her, did you not?

CONSTANT
> That's true; a husband is scarce to be borne upon any terms,
> much less when he fights with his wife. Methinks she should
> e'en have cuckolded him upon the very spot, to show that
> after the battle she was master of the field.   30

HEARTFREE
> A council of war of women would infallibly have advised
> her to't. But, I confess, so agreeable a woman as Bellinda
> deserves a better usage.

CONSTANT
> Bellinda again!

HEARTFREE
> My lady, I mean. What a pox makes me blunder so today?—   35
> (*Aside*) A plague of this treacherous tongue!

CONSTANT
> Prithee, look upon me seriously, Heartfree.—Now answer
> me directly: is it my lady, or Bellinda, employs your careful
> thoughts thus?

HEARTFREE
> My lady, or Bellinda?   40

CONSTANT
> In love! by this light, in love!

HEARTFREE
> In love?

CONSTANT
> Nay, ne'er deny it; for thou'lt do it so awkwardly, 'twill but

make the jest sit heavier about thee. My dear friend, I give
thee much joy.   45

HEARTFREE

Why prithee, you won't persuade me to it, will you?

CONSTANT

That she's mistress of your tongue, that's plain; and I know
you are so honest a fellow, your tongue and heart always go
together. But how—but how the devil—? Pha ha ha ha!—

HEARTFREE

Hey-day! Why, sure you don't believe it in earnest?   50

CONSTANT

Yes, I do; because I see you deny it in jest.

HEARTFREE

Nay, but look you, Ned—a—deny in jest—a—Gadzooks!
you know I say—a—when a man denies a thing in jest—a—

CONSTANT

Pha ha ha ha ha!

HEARTFREE

—Nay, then we shall have it. What, because a man stumbles   55
at a word? Did you never make a blunder?

CONSTANT

Yes, for I am in love; I own it.

HEARTFREE

Then, so am I! (*Embracing him*) Now laugh till thy soul's
glutted with mirth!—But, dear Constant, don't tell the
town on't.   60

CONSTANT

Nay then, 'twere almost pity to laugh at thee after so honest
a confession. But tell us a little, Jack; by what new-invented
arms has this mighty stroke been given?

HEARTFREE

E'en by that unaccountable weapon called *je ne sais quoi*; for
everything that can come within the verge of beauty, I have   65
seen it with indifference.

CONSTANT

So in few words, then, the *je ne sais quoi* has been too hard
for the quilted petticoat.

HEARTFREE

Egad, I think the *je ne sais quoi* is in the quilted petticoat; at
least, 'tis certain I ne'er think on't without—a—a *je ne sais*   70
quoi in every part about me.

---

64 *je ne sais quoi* I know not what, i.e., an indefinable attraction or 'certain
   something'

CONSTANT

Well; but have all your remedies lost their virtue? have you turned her inside out yet?

HEARTFREE

I dare not so much as think on't.

CONSTANT

But don't the two years' fatigue I have had discourage you?   75

HEARTFREE

Yes; I dread what I foresee, yet cannot quit the enterprise— like some soldiers whose courage dwells more in their honour than their nature: on they go, though the body trembles at what the soul makes it undertake.

CONSTANT

Nay, if you expect your mistress will use you as your pro-   80
fanations against her sex deserve, you tremble justly. But how do you intend to proceed, friend?

HEARTFREE

Thou know'st I'm but a novice; be friendly, and advise me.

CONSTANT

Why, look you then; I'd have you—serenade, and a—write a song—go to church—look like a fool—be very officious—   85
ogle—write—and lead out; and who knows but in a year or two's time you may be—called a troublesome puppy and sent about your business.

HEARTFREE

That's hard.

CONSTANT

Yet thus it oft falls out with lovers, sir.   90

HEARTFREE

Pox on me for making one of the number!

CONSTANT

Have a care! Say no saucy things; 'twill but augment your crime and, if your mistress hears on't, increase your punishment.

HEARTFREE

Prithee, say something then to encourage me; you know I   95
helped you in your distress.

CONSTANT

Why then, to encourage you to perseverance that you may be thoroughly ill-used for your offences, I'll put you in mind that even the coyest ladies of 'em all are made up of desires, as well as we; and though they do hold out a long   100

_____

86 *lead out* to escort a lady from the theatre to her coach after the play; Lord Foppington spends a whole hour 'leading 'em out' in *The Relapse* (II.i.236)

time, they will capitulate at last. For that thundering
engineer, nature, does make such havoc in the town, they
must surrender at long run or perish in their own flames.

Enter a FOOTMAN

[FOOTMAN (*To* CONSTANT)]
Sir, there's a porter without with a letter; he desires to give
it into your own hands.   105
CONSTANT
Call him in.   [*Exit* FOOTMAN]

Enter PORTER

What, Jo! Is it thee?
PORTER
An't please you, sir, I was ordered to deliver this into your
own hands, by two well-shaped ladies at the New Exchange.
I was at your honour's lodgings, and your servants sent me   110
hither.
CONSTANT
'Tis well. Are you to carry any answer?
PORTER
No, my noble master. They gave me my orders and whip!
they were gone, like a maidenhead at fifteen.
CONSTANT
Very well; there.   (*Gives him money*) 115
PORTER
God bless your honour.   (*Exit* PORTER)
CONSTANT
Now let's see what honest trusty Jo has brought us.—
(*Reads*) 'If you and your playfellow can spare time from
your business and devotions, don't fail·to be at Spring
Garden about eight in the evening. You'll find nothing there   120
but women, so you need bring no other arms than what you
usually carry about you'.—So, playfellow, here's something
to stay your stomach till your mistress's dish is ready for
you.
HEARTFREE
Some of our old battered acquaintance. I won't go, not I.   125
CONSTANT
Nay, that you can't avoid. There's honour in the case; 'tis a
challenge, and I want a second.

113 *whip!* presto!

---

107 *Jo!* To assist Constant's memory, each porter's name was stamped on
    a ticket at his belt.
109 *New Exchange* a fashionable shopping arcade in the Strand

HEARTFREE

I doubt I shall be but a very useless one to you; for I'm so disheartened by this wound Bellinda has given me, I don't think I shall have courage enough to draw my sword.   130

CONSTANT

Oh, if that be all, come along; I'll warrant you find sword enough for such enemies as we have to deal withal.   (*Exeunt*)

Act IV, Scene iii

Enter CONSTABLE *&c., with* SIR JOHN

CONSTABLE

Come along, sir; I thought to have let you slip this morning, because you were a minister; but you are as drunk and as abusive as ever. We'll see what the justice of the peace will say to you.

SIR JOHN

And you shall see what I'll sav to the justice of the peace,   5
sirrah.   (*They knock at the door*)

Enter SERVANT

CONSTABLE

Pray acquaint his worship, we have got an unruly parson here. We are unwilling to expose him, but don't know what to do with him.

SERVANT

I'll acquaint my master.   (*Exit* SERVANT)   10

SIR JOHN

You—constable—what damned justice is this?

CONSTABLE

One that will take care of you, I warrant you.

Enter JUSTICE

JUSTICE

Well, Mr Constable, what's the disorder here?

CONSTABLE

An't please your worship—

---

s.d. *Enter* CONSTABLE ... Q1 continues without any break here, but clearly the scene has changed to the Justice's house, or the street outside it.

SIR JOHN

Let me speak, and be damned; I'm a divine, and can unfold   15
mysteries better than you can do.

JUSTICE

Sadness, sadness, a minister so overtaken!—Pray, sir, give
the constable leave to speak, and I'll hear you very patiently;
I assure you, sir, I will.

SIR JOHN

Sir—you are a very civil magistrate. Your most humble   20
servant.

CONSTABLE

An't please your worship, then, he has attempted to beat the
watch tonight, and swore—

SIR JOHN

You lie!

JUSTICE

Hold, pray sir, a little.   25

SIR JOHN

Sir, your very humble servant.

CONSTABLE

Indeed, sir, he came at us without any provocation, called
us whores and rogues, and laid us on with a great quarter-
staff. He was in my Lord Rake's company; they have been
playing the devil tonight.   30

JUSTICE

Hem, hem.—Pray sir, may you be chaplain to my lord?

SIR JOHN

Sir—I presume—I may if I will.

JUSTICE

My meaning, sir, is: are you so?

SIR JOHN

Sir—you mean very well.

JUSTICE

He hem, hem.—Under favour, sir, pray answer me directly.   35

SIR JOHN

Under favour, sir—do you use to answer directly when you
are drunk?

JUSTICE

Good lack, good lack! Here's nothing to be got from him.—
Pray, sir, may I crave your name?

SIR JOHN

Sir—my name's—(*He hiccups*) Hiccup, sir.   40

---

17 *overtaken* drunk
28 *laid us on* assailed us

JUSTICE
Hiccup? Doctor Hiccup, I have known a great many country
parsons of that name, especially down in the Fens. Pray
where do you live, sir?

SIR JOHN
Here—and there, sir.

JUSTICE
Why, what a strange man is this!—Where do you preach,   45
sir? Have you any cure?

SIR JOHN
Sir—I have—a very good cure—for a clap, at your service.

JUSTICE
Lord have mercy upon us!

SIR JOHN (*Aside*)
This fellow does ask so many impertinent questions, I
believe, egad, 'tis the justice's wife in the justice's clothes.   50

JUSTICE
Mr Constable, I vow and protest I don't know what to do
with him.

CONSTABLE
Truly, he has been but a troublesome guest to us all night.

JUSTICE
I think I had e'en best let him go about his business, for I'm
unwilling to expose him.   55

CONSTABLE
E'en what your worship thinks fit.

SIR JOHN
Sir—not to interrupt, Mr Constable—I have a small favour
to ask.

JUSTICE
Sir, I open both my ears to you.

SIR JOHN
Sir, your very humble servant. I have a little urgent business   60
calls upon me; and therefore I desire the favour of you to
bring matters to a conclusion.

JUSTICE
Sir, if I were sure that business were not to commit more
disorders, I would release you.

SIR JOHN
None—by my priesthood!   65

JUSTICE
Then, Mr Constable, you may discharge him.

---

42 *the Fens* marshy, low-lying districts in Cambridgeshire, Lincolnshire,
and some adjoining counties

SIR JOHN
Sir, your very humble servant. If you please to accept of a
bottle—
JUSTICE
I thank you kindly, sir; but I never drink in a morning.
Good-bye to ye, sir, good-bye to ye.   70
SIR JOHN
Good-bye t'ye, good sir. (*Exit* JUSTICE) So.—Now, Mr
Constable, shall you and I go pick up a whore together?
CONSTABLE
No, thank you, sir; my wife's enough to satisfy any reason-
able man.
SIR JOHN
(*Aside*) He he he he he!—the fool is married, then.—   75
[*Aloud*] Well, you won't go?
CONSTABLE
Not I, truly.
SIR JOHN
Then I'll go by myself; and you and your wife may be
damned.   (*Exit* SIR JOHN)
CONSTABLE (*Gazing after him*)
Why, God a mercy, parson!   (*Exeunt*)   80

Act IV, Scene iv

Spring Garden
CONSTANT *and* HEARTFREE *cross the stage*

CONSTANT
So. I think we are about the time appointed; let us walk up
this way.

Exeunt. As they go off, enter LADY FANCYFULL *and*
MADAMOISELLE, *masked and dogging 'em*

LADY FANCYFULL
Good. Thus far I have dogged 'em without being discovered.
'Tis infallibly some intrigue that brings them to Spring
Garden. How my poor heart is torn and racked with fear   5
and jealousy! Yet let it be anything but that flirt Bellinda,
and I'll try to bear it. But if it prove her, all that's woman in
me shall be employed to destroy her.
                (*Exeunt after* CONSTANT *and* HEARTFREE)

80 *God a mercy* thank you (ironic)
   2 s.d. *As ... dogging 'em* Q1 prints this immediately before Constant's
   line

Re-enter CONSTANT *and* HEARTFREE, LADY FANCYFULL *and*
MADAMOISELLE *still following at a distance*

CONSTANT
I see no females yet that have anything to say to us. I'm
afraid we are bantered.   10
HEARTFREE
I wish we were, for I'm in no humour to make either them
or myself merry.
CONSTANT
Nay, I'm sure you'll make them merry enough, if I tell 'em
why you are dull. But prithee, why so heavy and sad before
you begin to be ill-used?   15
HEARTFREE
For the same reason, perhaps, that you are so brisk and well
pleased: because both pains and pleasures are generally more
considerable in prospect than when they come to pass.

Enter LADY BRUTE *and* BELLINDA, *masked and poorly
dressed*

CONSTANT
How now, who are these? Not our game, I hope.
HEARTFREE
If they are, we are e'en well enough served, to come hunting   20
here when we had so much better game in chase elsewhere.
LADY FANCYFULL (*To* MADAMOISELLE)
So; those are their ladies, without doubt. But I'm afraid that
doily stuff is not worn for want of better clothes. They are
the very shape and size of Bellinda and her aunt.
MADAMOISELLE
So day be inteed, matam.   25
LADY FANCYFULL
We'll slip into this close arbour, where we may hear all they
say.   (*Exeunt* LADY FANCYFULL *and* MADAMOISELLE)
LADY BRUTE
What, are you afraid of us, gentlemen?
HEARTFREE
Why truly, I think we may, if appearance don't lie.

10 *bantered* (1) cheated, tricked (2) made fun of
20 *hunting* Q1–3 (a hunting P)

18 s.d. *masked* Masks were rarely worn by respectable women at this
period.
23 *doily stuff* summer-weight woollen cloth, named after Thomas Doyly, a
London draper specializing in 'such Stuffs as might at once be cheap
and genteel' (the *Spectator*, no. 283, 24 January 1712)

BELLINDA

Do you always find women what they appear to be, sir?   30

HEARTFREE

No, forsooth; but I seldom find 'em better than they appear
to be.

BELLINDA

Then the outside's best, you think?

HEARTFREE

'Tis the honestest.

CONSTANT

Have a care, Heartfree; you are relapsing again.   35

LADY BRUTE

Why, does the gentleman use to rail at women?

CONSTANT

He has done formerly.

BELLINDA

I suppose he had very good cause for't.—They did not use
you so well as you thought you deserved, sir.

LADY BRUTE

They made themselves merry at your expense, sir.   40

BELLINDA

Laughed when you sighed.

LADY BRUTE

Slept while you were waking.

BELLINDA

Had your porter beat.

LADY BRUTE

And threw your *billets-doux* in the fire.

HEARTFREE

Hey-day, I shall do more than rail presently.   45

BELLINDA

Why, you won't beat us, will you?

HEARTFREE

I don't know but I may.

CONSTANT

What the devil's coming here? Sir John in a gown?—And
drunk, i'faith.

Enter SIR JOHN

SIR JOHN

What a pox! Here's Constant, Heartfree—and two whores,   50
egad!—O you covetous rogues! what, have you never a
spare punk for your friend? But I'll share with you.

(*He seizes both the women*)

44 *billets-doux* ed. (billet-doux Q1–3, P) love-letters

HEARTFREE

Why, what the plague have you been doing, knight?

SIR JOHN

Why, I have been beating the watch, and scandalizing the
clergy.   55

HEARTFREE

A very good account, truly.

SIR JOHN

And what do you think I'll do next?

CONSTANT

Nay, that no man can guess.

SIR JOHN

Why, if you'll let me sup with you, I'll treat both your
strumpets.   60

LADY BRUTE (*Aside*)

O Lord, we are undone!

HEARTFREE

No, we can't sup together, because we have some affairs
elsewhere. But if you'll accept of these two ladies, we'll be so
complaisant to you to resign our right in 'em.

BELLINDA (*Aside*)

Lord, what shall we do?   65

SIR JOHN

Let me see; their clothes are such damned clothes they won't
pawn for the reckoning.

HEARTFREE

Sir John, your servant. Rapture attend you!

CONSTANT

Adieu, ladies; make much of the gentleman.

LADY BRUTE

Why, sure, you won't leave us in the hands of a drunken   70
fellow to abuse us?

SIR JOHN

Who do you call a drunken fellow, you slut you? I'm a man
of quality; the king has made me a knight.

HEARTFREE

Ay, ay, you are in good hands! Adieu, adieu!

(HEARTFREE *runs off*)

LADY BRUTE

The devil's hands! Let me go, or I'll—for heaven's sake,   75
protect us!

(*She breaks from him, runs to* CONSTANT, *twitching off her
mask and clapping it on again*)

74 s.d. (HEARTFREE *runs off*) Q1 prints this before Heartfree's line

SIR JOHN
I'll devil you, you jade you! I'll demolish your ugly face!
CONSTANT
Hold a little, knight; she swoons.
SIR JOHN
I'll swoon her!
CONSTANT
Hey, Heartfree!   80

Re-enter HEARTFREE. BELLINDA *runs to him and shows her*
face

HEARTFREE
O heavens! My dear creature, stand there a little.
CONSTANT [*To* HEARTFREE, *aside*]
Pull him off, Jack.
HEARTFREE
Hold, mighty man; look you, sir, we did but jest with you.
These are ladies of our acquaintance that we had a mind to
frighten a little, but now you must leave us.   85
SIR JOHN
Oons, I won't leave you, not I!
HEARTFREE
Nay, but you must, though; and therefore make no words
on't.
SIR JOHN
Then you are a couple of damned uncivil fellows. And I
hope your punks will give you sauce to your mutton!   90
                                                    (*Exit* SIR JOHN)
LADY BRUTE
Oh, I shall never come to myself again, I'm so frightened!
CONSTANT
'Twas a narrow 'scape, indeed.
BELLINDA
Women must have frolics, you see, whatever they cost 'em.
HEARTFREE
This might have proved a dear one, though.
LADY BRUTE
You are the more obliged to us, for the risk we run upon   95
your accounts.
CONSTANT
And I hope you'll acknowledge something due to our knight-

90 *sauce* venereal disease (slang)
90 *mutton* prostitute (slang)
93 *must* Q1–3 (must needs P)

errantry, ladies. This is the second time we have delivered
you.
LADY BRUTE
'Tis true; and since we see fate has designed you for our   100
guardians, 'twill make us the more willing to trust ourselves
in your hands. But you must not have the worse opinion of
us for our innocent frolic.
HEARTFREE
Ladies, you may command our opinions in everything that
is to your advantage.   105
BELLINDA
Then, sir, I command you to be of opinion that women are
sometimes better than they appear to be.
                    (LADY BRUTE *and* CONSTANT *talk apart*)
HEARTFREE
Madam, you have made a convert of me in everything. I'm
grown a fool: I could be fond of a woman.
BELLINDA
I thank you, sir, in the name of the whole sex.   110
HEARTFREE
Which sex nothing but yourself could ever have atoned for.
BELLINDA
Now has my vanity a devilish itch, to know in what my merit
consists.
HEARTFREE
In your humility, madam, that keeps you ignorant it con-
sists at all.   115
BELLINDA
One other compliment with that serious face, and I hate you
for ever after.
HEARTFREE
Some women love to be abused; is that it you would be at?
BELLINDA
No, not that neither; but I'd have men talk plainly what's
fit for women to hear, without putting 'em either to a real, 120
or an affected blush.
HEARTFREE
Why then, in as plain terms as I can find to express myself,
I could love you even to—matrimony itself almost, egad.
BELLINDA
Just as Sir John did her ladyship there. What think you?
Don't you believe one month's time might bring you down   125
to the same indifference, only clad in a little better manners,

114–15 *consists* exists

perhaps? Well, you men are unaccountable things; mad till
you have your mistresses, and then stark mad till you are
rid of 'em again. Tell me honestly, is not your patience put
to a much severer trial after possession than before?   130

HEARTFREE

With a great many I must confess it is, to our eternal scandal;
but I—dear creature, do but try me!

BELLINDA

That's the surest way indeed to know, but not the safest.—
(*To* LADY BRUTE) Madam, are not you for taking a turn in the
Great Walk? It's almost dark; nobody will know us.   135

LADY BRUTE

Really, I find myself something idle, Bellinda; besides, I dote
upon this little odd private corner. But don't let my lazy
fancy confine you.

CONSTANT (*Aside*)

So, she would be left alone with me; that's well.

BELLINDA

Well, we'll take one turn and come to you again.—(*To*   140
HEARTFREE) Come, sir; shall we go pry into the secrets of the
garden? Who knows what discoveries we may make!

HEARTFREE

Madam, I'm at your service.

CONSTANT (*To* HEARTFREE, *aside*)

Don't make too much haste back, for—d'ye hear?—I may
be busy.   145

HEARTFREE

Enough.   ([*Exeunt*] BELLINDA *and* HEARTFREE)

LADY BRUTE

Sure you think me scandalously free, Mr Constant. I'm
afraid I shall lose your good opinion of me.

CONSTANT

My good opinion, madam, is like your cruelty, never to be
removed.   150

LADY BRUTE

But if I should remove my cruelty, then there's an end of
your good opinion.

---

146 s.d. [*Exeunt*] ed. (*Exit* Q1–3, P)

134–5 *a turn ... Walk* 'Ladies that have an Inclination to be Private, take
   Delight in the Close Walks of *Spring-Gardens*, where both Sexes meet,
   and mutually serve one another as Guides to lose their Way' (Tom
   Brown, *Amusements* (1700), p. 54).

CONSTANT

There is not so strict an alliance between 'em, neither. 'Tis
certain I should love you then better (if that be possible)
than I do now; and where I love, I always esteem.   155

LADY BRUTE

Indeed, I doubt you much. Why, suppose you had a wife,
and she should entertain a gallant?

CONSTANT

If I gave her just cause, how could I justly condemn her?

LADY BRUTE

Ah, but you'd differ widely about just causes.

CONSTANT

But blows can bear no dispute.   160

LADY BRUTE

Nor ill manners much, truly.

CONSTANT

Then no woman upon earth has so just a cause as you have.

LADY BRUTE

Oh, but a faithful wife is a beautiful character.

CONSTANT

To a deserving husband, I confess it is.

LADY BRUTE

But can his faults release my duty?   165

CONSTANT

In equity, without doubt. And where laws dispense with
equity, equity should dispense with laws.

LADY BRUTE

Pray, let's leave this dispute; for you men have as much
witchcraft in your arguments as women have in their eyes.

CONSTANT

But whilst you attack me with your charms, 'tis but reason-   170
able I assault you with mine.

LADY BRUTE

The case is not the same. What mischief we do, we can't
help, and therefore are to be forgiven.

CONSTANT

Beauty soon obtains pardon for the pain that it gives, when
it applies the balm of compassion to the wound; but a fine   175
face and a hard heart is almost as bad as an ugly face and
a soft one—both very troublesome to many a poor gentleman.

LADY BRUTE

Yes, and to many a poor gentlewoman, too, I can assure you.
But pray, which of 'em is it that most afflicts you?

---

166 *equity* See note to I.i.95–6.

CONSTANT

Your glass and conscience will inform you, madam. But for   180
heaven's sake (for now I must be serious), if pity or if
gratitude can move you (*Taking her hand*), if constancy and
truth have power to tempt you, if love, if adoration can affect
you, give me at least some hopes that time may do what you
perhaps mean never to perform; 'twill ease my sufferings,   185
though not quench my flame.

LADY BRUTE

Your sufferings eased, your flame would soon abate; and
that I would preserve, not quench it, sir.

CONSTANT

Would you preserve it, nourish it with favours; for that's
the food it naturally requires.   190

LADY BRUTE

Yet on that natural food 'twould surfeit soon, should I
resolve to grant all that you would ask.

CONSTANT

And in refusing all, you starve it. Forgive me, therefore,
since my hunger rages, if I at last grow wild and in my
frenzy force at least this from you. (*Kissing her hand*) Or if   195
you'd have my flame soar higher still, then grant me this,
and this, and this, and thousands more. (*Kissing first her
hand, then her neck.—Aside*) For now's the time; she melts
into compassion.

LADY BRUTE

(*Aside*) Poor coward virtue, how it shuns the battle.—   200
[*Aloud*] O heavens! let me go.

CONSTANT

Ay, go, ay. Where shall we go, my charming angel?—Into
this private arbour.—Nay, let's lose no time—moments are
precious.

LADY BRUTE

And lovers wild. Pray let us stop here; at least for this time. 205

CONSTANT

'Tis impossible. He that has power over you can have none
over himself.

LADY BRUTE

Ah, I'm lost!

> *As he is forcing her into the arbour,* LADY FANCYFULL *and*
> MADAMOISELLE *bolt out upon them, and run over the stage*

LADY FANCYFULL
   Fie fie fie fie fie!
MADAMOISELLE
   Fie fie fie fie fie!   210
             [*Exeunt* LADY FANCYFULL *and* MADAMOISELLE]
CONSTANT
   Death and furies! who are these?
LADY BRUTE
   O heavens! I'm out of my wits. If they knew me, I'm ruined.
CONSTANT
   Don't be frightened; ten thousand to one they are strangers
   to you.
LADY BRUTE
   Whatever they are, I won't stay here a moment longer.   215
CONSTANT
   Whither will you go?
LADY BRUTE
   Home, as if the devil were in me. Lord, where's this Bellinda
   now?

                Enter BELLINDA *and* HEARTFREE

   Oh, it's well you are come. I'm so frightened my hair stands
   on end. Let's be gone, for heaven's sake!   220
BELLINDA
   Lord, what's the matter?
LADY BRUTE
   The devil's the matter: we are discovered. Here's a couple
   of women have done the most impertinent thing. Away,
   away, away, away, away!
             (*Exit running* [*with* BELLINDA. *The men follow*])

          Re-enter LADY FANCYFULL *and* MADAMOISELLE

LADY FANCYFULL
   Well, Madamoiselle, 'tis a prodigious thing how women   225
   can suffer filthy fellows to grow so familiar with 'em.
MADAMOISELLE
   Ah, matam, *il n'y a rien de si naturel.*

220 *on end* ed. (an end Q1–3, P, the older form)
227 *il . . . naturel* there's nothing more natural

222–3 *Here's . . . thing* Lady Fancyfull and Madamoiselle, or Lady Brute
   and Bellinda?

LADY FANCYFULL
Fie fie fie! But oh, my heart! O jealousy! O torture! I'm
upon the rack. What shall I do? My lover's lost; I ne'er shall
see him mine.—(*Pausing*) But I may be revenged, and that's   230
the same thing. Ah, sweet revenge! Thou welcome thought,
thou healing balsam to my wounded soul! Be but propitious
on this one occasion, I'll place my heaven in thee for all my
life to come.

    To woman, how indulgent nature's kind!   235
    No blast of fortune long disturbs her mind.
    Compliance to her fate supports her still;
    If love won't make her happy—mischief will.   (*Exeunt*)

Act V, Scene i

LADY FANCYFULL's *House*
Enter LADY FANCYFULL *and* MADAMOISELLE

LADY FANCYFULL
Well, Madamoiselle; did you dog the filthy things?
MADAMOISELLE
O que oui, matam.
LADY FANCYFULL
And where are they?
MADAMOISELLE
Au logis.
LADY FANCYFULL
What, men and all?   5
MADAMOISELLE
Tous ensemble.
LADY FANCYFULL
Oh, confidence! What, carry their fellows to their own
house?
MADAMOISELLE
C'est que le mari n'y est pas.
LADY FANCYFULL
No, so I believe, truly. But he shall be there, and quickly   10
too, if I can find him out. Well, 'tis a prodigious thing, to see
when men and women get together, how they fortify one

238 s.d. (*Exeunt*) Q1 follows this with 'The End of the Fourth Act'.
  2 *O que oui* Yes indeed
  4 *Au logis* At home
  6 *Tous ensemble* All of them together
  9 *C'est . . . pas* It's because the husband is not there

another in their impudence. But if that drunken fool, her
husband, be to be found in e'er a tavern in town, I'll send him
amongst 'em. I'll spoil their sport!   15

MADAMOISELLE
En vérité, matam, *ce serait dommage.*

LADY FANCYFULL
'Tis in vain to oppose it, Madamoiselle; therefore never go
about it. For I am the steadiest creature in the world—when
I have determined to do mischief. So, come along. (*Exeunt*)

Act V, Scene ii

SIR JOHN BRUTE'*s House*
Enter CONSTANT, HEARTFREE, LADY BRUTE, BELLINDA *and*
LOVEWELL

LADY BRUTE
But are you sure you don't mistake, Lovewell?

LOVEWELL
Madam, I saw 'em all go into the tavern together, and my
master was so drunk he could scarce stand.   [*Exit*]

LADY BRUTE
Then, gentlemen, I believe we may venture to let you stay
and play at cards with us an hour or two; for they'll scarce   5
part till morning.

BELLINDA
I think 'tis pity they should ever part.

CONSTANT
The company that's here, madam.

LADY BRUTE
Then, sir, the company that's here must remember to part
itself, in time.   10

CONSTANT
Madam, we don't intend to forfeit your future favours by
an indiscreet usage of this. The moment you give us the
signal, we shan't fail to make our retreat.

LADY BRUTE
Upon those conditions, then, let us sit down to cards.

Enter LOVEWELL

16 *En . . . dommage* In truth, matam, it would be a pity
7 *pity* Q1–3 (a pity P)
12 *an indiscreet* Q1–2 (indiscreet Q3, P)

[LOVEWELL]

O Lord, madam, here's my master just staggering in upon   15
you! He has been quarrelsome yonder, and they have kicked
him out of the company.   [*Exit*]

LADY BRUTE

Into the closet, gentlemen, for heaven's sake! I'll wheedle
him to bed, if possible.

(CONSTANT *and* HEARTFREE *run into the closet*)

Enter SIR JOHN, *all dirt and bloody*

Ah—ah—he's all over blood!   20

SIR JOHN

What the plague does the woman—squall for? Did you
never see a man in pickle before?

LADY BRUTE

Lord, where have you been?

SIR JOHN

I have been at—cuffs.

LADY BRUTE

I fear that is not all. I hope you are not wounded.   25

SIR JOHN

Sound as a roach, wife.

LADY BRUTE

I'm mighty glad to hear it.

SIR JOHN

You know—I think you lie.

LADY BRUTE

I know you do me wrong to think so, then. For heaven's my
witness, I had rather see my own blood trickle down than   30
yours.

SIR JOHN

Then will I be crucified.

LADY BRUTE

'Tis a hard fate I should not be believed.

SIR JOHN

'Tis a damned atheistical age, wife.

LADY BRUTE

I am sure I have given you a thousand tender proofs, how   35
great my care is of you. Nay, spite of all your cruel thoughts

29 *I know you* Q1–3 (You P)
29 *so, then* Q1–3 (so P)
36 *Nay* Q1–3 (But P)

---

26 proverbial (Tilley, R 143); the roach is a fresh-water fish traditionally
thought incapable of disease

I'll still persist, and at this moment, if I can, persuade you
to lie down and sleep a little.

SIR JOHN
Why—do you think I am drunk—you slut you?

LADY BRUTE
Heaven forbid I should! But I'm afraid you are feverish.   40
Pray let me feel your pulse.

SIR JOHN
Stand off, and be damned.

LADY BRUTE
Why, I see your distemper in your very eyes. You are all on
fire. Pray, go to bed; let me entreat you.

SIR JOHN
—Come kiss me, then.   45

LADY BRUTE (*Kissing him*)
There: now go.—(*Aside*) He stinks like poison.

SIR JOHN
I see it goes damnably against your stomach—and therefore
—kiss me again.

LADY BRUTE
Nay, now you fool me.

SIR JOHN
Do't, I say.   50

LADY BRUTE
(*Aside*) Ah, Lord have mercy upon me!—[*Kissing him*] Well,
there: now will you go?

SIR JOHN
Now, wife, you shall see my gratitude. You give me two
kisses—I'll give you—two hundred. (*Kisses and tumbles her*)

LADY BRUTE
O Lord! Pray, Sir John, be quiet. Heavens, what a pickle   55
am I in!

BELLINDA (*Aside*)
If I were in her pickle, I'd call my gallant out of tne closet,
and he should cudgel him soundly.

SIR JOHN
So; now, you being as dirty and as nasty as myself, we may
go pig together. But first I must have a cup of your cold tea,   60
wife.   (*Going to the closet*)

50 *Do't* Q1–2, P(Don't Q3)   59 *nasty* repulsively filthy
60 *pig together* lie together in one bed (slang)

---

60 *cold tea* prepared in advance for occasional drinking and, to judge from
William Burnaby's *The Reformed Wife* (1700), still so fashionable it
was imitated by tradesmen's wives (II.i.80)

LADY BRUTE

[*Aside*] Oh, I'm ruined!—[*Aloud*] There's none there, my dear.

SIR JOHN

I'll warrant you I'll find some, my dear.

LADY BRUTE

You can't open the door; the lock's spoiled. I have been   65
turning and turning the key this half-hour to no purpose.
I'll send for the smith tomorrow.

SIR JOHN

There's ne'er a smith in Europe can open a door with more
expedition than I can do.—As for example—pou! (*He bursts
open the door with his foot*)—How now? What the devil have   70
we got here?—Constant!—Heartfree!—and the two whores
again, egad!—This is the worst cold tea—that ever I met
with in my life.

Enter CONSTANT *and* HEARTFREE

LADY BRUTE (*Aside*)

O Lord, what will become of us?

SIR JOHN

Gentlemen—I am your very humble servant—I give you   75
many thanks—I see you take care of my family—I shall do
all I can to return the obligation.

CONSTANT

Sir, how oddly soever this business may appear to you, you
would have no cause to be uneasy if you knew the truth of all
things; your lady is the most virtuous woman in the world,   80
and nothing has passed but an innocent frolic.

HEARTFREE

Nothing else, upon my honour, sir.

SIR JOHN

You are both very civil gentlemen—and my wife, there, is
a very civil gentlewoman; therefore I don't doubt but many
civil things have passed between you. Your very humble   85
servant.

LADY BRUTE (*Aside, to* CONSTANT)

Pray be gone; he's so drunk he can't hurt us tonight, and
tomorrow morning you shall hear from us.

CONSTANT

I'll obey you, madam.—[*Aloud*] Sir, when you are cool
you'll understand reason better; so then I shall take the   90
pains to inform you. If not—I wear a sword, sir, and so good-
bye to you.—Come along, Heartfree.

[*Exeunt* CONSTANT *and* HEARTFREE]

SIR JOHN
Wear a sword, sir? And what of all that, sir?—He comes to
my house, eats my meat, lies with my wife, dishonours my
family, gets a bastard to inherit my estate, and when I ask a   95
civil account of all this—Sir, says he, I wear a sword!—
Wear a sword, sir? Yes sir, says he, I wear a sword!—It may
be a good answer at cross-purposes, but 'tis a damned one
to a man in my whimsical circumstance.—Sir, says he, I
wear a sword!—(*To* LADY BRUTE) And what do you wear   100
now, ha? Tell me. (*Sitting down in a great chair*) What! You
are modest, and can't? Why then, I'll tell you, you slut
you. You wear—an impudent lewd face—a damned
designing heart—and a tail—and a tail full of—
                              (*He falls fast asleep, snoring*)

LADY BRUTE
So; thanks to kind heaven, he's fast for some hours.   105

BELLINDA
'Tis well he is so, that we may have time to lay our story
handsomely; for we must lie like the devil to bring ourselves
off.

LADY BRUTE
What shall we say, Bellinda?

BELLINDA (*Musing*)
I'll tell you: it must all light upon Heartfree and I. We'll   110
say he has courted me some time, but for reasons unknown
to us has ever been very earnest the thing might be kept
from Sir John; that therefore hearing him upon the stairs,
he run into the closet, though against our will, and Constant
with him, to prevent jealousy. And to give this a good im-   115
pudent face of truth (that I may deliver you from the trouble
you are in), I'll e'en (if he pleases) marry him.

LADY BRUTE
I'm beholding to you, cousin; but that would be carrying
the jest a little too far for your own sake. You know he's a
younger brother, and has nothing.   120

BELLINDA
'Tis true; but I like him, and have fortune enough to keep
above extremity. I can't say I would live with him in a cell
upon love and bread and butter; but I had rather have the

104 *tail* pudendum (slang)
118 *beholding* Q1–3 (beholden P)

---

98 *cross-purposes* a parlour game in which questions are linked to inappro-
   priate answers, with ludicrous results; it made Pepys 'mighty merry'
   (*Diary*, 26 December 1666)

man I love, and a middle state of life, than that gentleman
in the chair there, and twice your ladyship's splendour.   125
LADY BRUTE
In truth, niece, you are in the right on't; for I am very
uneasy with my ambition. But perhaps, had I married as
you'll do, I might have been as ill-used.
BELLINDA
Some risk, I do confess, there always is; but if a man has
the least spark either of honour or good nature, he can never   130
use a woman ill that loves him and makes his fortune both.
Yet I must own to you, some little struggling I still have with
this teasing ambition of ours; for pride, you know, is as
natural to a woman as 'tis to a saint. I can't help being fond
of this rogue; and yet it goes to my heart to think I must   135
never whisk to Hyde Park with above a pair of horses, have
no coronet upon my coach, nor a page to carry up my train.
But above all, that business of place—. Well, taking place
is a noble prerogative.
LADY BRUTE
Especially after a quarrel.   140
BELLINDA
Or of a rival. But pray say no more on't, for fear I change my
mind. For o'my conscience, were't not for your affair in the
balance, I should go near to pick up some odious man of
quality yet, and only take poor Heartfree for a gallant.
LADY BRUTE
Then him you must have, however things go?   145
BELLINDA
Yes.
LADY BRUTE
Why, we may pretend what we will, but 'tis a hard matter
to live without the man we love.
BELLINDA
Especially when we are married to the man we hate. Pray
tell me, do the men of the town ever believe us virtuous,   150
when they see us do so?
LADY BRUTE
Oh, no; nor indeed hardly, let us do what we will. They
most of 'em think there is no such thing as virtue, considered
in the strictest notions of it; and therefore when you hear
'em say such a one is a woman of reputation, they only   155
mean she's a woman of discretion. For they consider we have
no more religion than they have, nor so much morality;

138 *place* social precedence

and between you and I, Bellinda, I'm afraid the want of
inclination seldom protects any of us.

BELLINDA

But what think you of the fear of being found out?   160

LADY BRUTE

I think that never kept any woman virtuous long. We are
not such cowards neither. No; let us once pass fifteen, and
we have too good an opinion of our own cunning to believe
the world can penetrate into what we would keep a secret.
And so, in short, we cannot reasonably blame the men for   165
judging of us by themselves.

BELLINDA

But sure we are not so wicked as they are, after all?

LADY BRUTE

We are as wicked, child, but our vice lies another way. Men
have more courage than we, so they commit more bold,
impudent sins. They quarrel, fight, swear, drink, blas-   170
pheme, and the like; whereas we, being cowards, only
backbite, tell lies, cheat at cards, and so forth.—But 'tis late.
Let's end our discourse for tonight, and out of an excess
of charity take a small care of that nasty drunken thing
there.—Do but look at him, Bellinda!   175

BELLINDA

Ah, 'tis a savoury dish.

LADY BRUTE

As savoury as 'tis, I'm cloyed with't. Prithee, call the butler
to take away.

BELLINDA

Call the butler? Call the scavenger!—(*To a servant within*)
Who's there? Call Rasor! Let him take away his master,   180
scour him clean with a little soap and sand, and so put him
to bed.

LADY BRUTE

Come, Bellinda, I'll e'en lie with you tonight; and in the
morning we'll send for our gentlemen to set this matter
even.   185

BELLINDA

With all my heart.

LADY BRUTE (*Making a low curtsy* [*to* SIR JOHN])
Good night, my dear.

---

178 *take* Q1–3 (take it P)   186 *With all* Q2–3, P (Withal Q1)

179 *scavenger* officer of a city ward answerable 'that the Ways, Streets, and
     Lanes, be cleansed of Dung, and all manner of Filth' (Thomas Delaune,
     Angliae Metropolis (1690), p. 248)

BOTH
   Ha ha ha!   (*Exeunt*)

Enter RASOR

[RASOR]
   My lady there's a wag—my master there's a cuckold.
   Marriage is a slippery thing; women have depraved appe-   190
   tites. My lady's a wag; I have heard all, I have seen all, I
   understand all—and I'll tell all, for my little Frenchwoman
   loves news dearly. This story'll gain her heart, or nothing
   will.—(*To his master*) Come, sir, your head's too full of fumes
   at present to make room for your jealousy; but I reckon   195
   we shall have rare work with you when your pate's empty.
   Come to your kennel, you cuckoldly drunken sot you!
                           (*Carries him out upon his back*)

Act V, Scene iii

LADY FANCYFULL's *House*
Enter LADY FANCYFULL *and* MADAMOISELLE

LADY FANCYFULL
   But why did not you tell me before, Madamoiselle, that
   Rasor and you were fond?
MADAMOISELLE
   De modesty hinder me, matam.
LADY FANCYFULL
   Why truly, modesty does often hinder us from doing things
   we have an extravagant mind to. But does he love you well   5
   enough yet, to do anything you bid him? Do you think to
   oblige you he would speak scandal?
MADAMOISELLE
   Matam, to oblige your ladyship he shall speak blasphemy.
LADY FANCYFULL
   Why then, Madamoiselle, I'll tell you what you shall do.
   You shall engage him to tell his master all that passed at   10
   Spring Garden: I have a mind he should know what a wife
   and a niece he has got.
MADAMOISELLE
   Il le fera, matam.

Enter a FOOTMAN, *who speaks to* MADAMOISELLE *apart*

13 *Il le fera* He'll do it

FOOTMAN
> Madamoiselle, yonder's Mr Rasor desires to speak with you.

MADAMOISELLE
> Tell him, I come presently. (*Exit* FOOTMAN)—Rasor be dare,   15
> matam.

LADY FANCYFULL
> That's fortunate. Well, I'll leave you together. And if you
> find him stubborn, Madamoiselle—hark you—don't refuse
> him a few little reasonable liberties to put him into humour.

MADAMOISELLE
> *Laissez-moi faire.*   (*Exit* LADY FANCYFULL)   20

> RASOR *peeps in, and seeing* LADY FANCYFULL *gone, runs to*
> MADAMOISELLE, *takes her about the neck and kisses her*

> How now, confidence!

RASOR
> How now, modesty!

MADAMOISELLE
> Who make you so familiar, sirrah?

RASOR
> My impudence, hussy.

MADAMOISELLE
> Stand off, rogue-face!   25

RASOR
> Ah, Madamoiselle, great news at our house!

MADAMOISELLE
> Wy, wat be de matter?

RASOR
> The matter? —Why, uptails-all's the matter!

MADAMOISELLE
> *Tu te moques de moi.*

RASOR
> Now do you long to know the particulars—the time when,   30
> the place where, the manner how. But I won't tell you a
> word more.

MADAMOISELLE
> Nay, den dou kill me, Rasor.

RASOR (*Clapping his hands behind him*)
> Come, kiss me, then.

20 *Laissez-moi faire* Just watch me
29 *Tu ... moi* You're laughing at me

---

28 *uptails-all* the name of a card game and an old song, used here as a
   slang term for (1) confusion, high jinks (2) copulation
30–1 *time ... how* terms which belong to a legal indictment

MADAMOISELLE

Nay, pridee tell me.   35

RASOR (*Going*)

Good-bye to ye!

MADAMOISELLE

Hold, hold! I will kiss dee.   (*Kissing him*)

RASOR

So; that's civil. Why now, my pretty poll, my goldfinch, my
little water-wagtail, you must know that—come, kiss me
again.   40

MADAMOISELLE

I won't kiss dee no more.

RASOR

Good-bye to ye!

MADAMOISELLE

Doucement. (*Kissing him*) Dare; *es-tu content?*

RASOR

So; now I'll tell thee all. Why the news is, that cuckoldom in
folio is newly printed, and matrimony in quarto is just going   45
into the press. Will you buy any books, Madamoiselle?

MADAMOISELLE

Tu parles comme un libraire; de devil no understand dee.

RASOR

Why then, that I may make myself intelligible to a waiting-
woman, I'll speak like a *valet de chambre.* My lady has
cuckolded my master.   50

MADAMOISELLE

Bon!

RASOR

Which we take very ill from her hands, I can tell her that.
We can't yet prove matter of fact upon her.

MADAMOISELLE

N'importe.

RASOR

But we can prove that matter of fact had like to have been   55
upon her.

38 *poll* ed. (pall Q1) talkative woman (slang)
39 *wagtail* prostitute (slang)
43 *Doucement . . . content?* Wait a minute . . . are you satisfied?
47 *Tu . . . libraire* You're talking like a bookseller
49 *valet de chambre* gentleman's gentleman
51 *Bon!* Good!
54 *N'importe* That doesn't matter

53 *matter of fact* another legal term loosely used here to distinguish
verifiable fact from probability or inference

MADAMOISELLE
Oui-dà!

RASOR
For we have such bloody circumstances—

MADAMOISELLE
Sans doute.

RASOR
That any man of parts may draw tickling conclusions from   60
'em.

MADAMOISELLE
Fort bien.

RASOR
We have found a couple of tight, well-built gentlemen
stuffed into her ladyship's closet.

MADAMOISELLE
Le diable!   65

RASOR
And I, in my particular person, have discovered a most
damnable plot how to persuade my poor master that all this
hide-and-seek, this will-in-the-wisp, has no other meaning
than a Christian marriage for sweet Mrs Bellinda.

MADAMOISELLE
Un marriage?—Ah, les drôlesses!   70

RASOR
Don't you interrupt me, hussy; 'tis agreed, I say. And my
innocent lady, to wriggle herself out at the back-door of the
business, turns marriage-bawd to her niece, and resolves to
deliver up her fair body to be tumbled and mumbled by that
young liquorish whipster, Heartfree. Now are you satisfied?   75

MADAMOISELLE
No.

RASOR
Right woman, always gaping for more!

MADAMOISELLE
Dis be all, den, dat dou know?

---

57 *Oui-dà!* To be sure!
59 *Sans doute* I dare say
62 *Fort bien* Very well
65 *Le diable!* The devil you have!
70 *Un . . . drôlesses!* (drôless Q1) A marriage?—Ah, the strumpets!
74 *mumbled* fondled with kisses
75 *liquorish whipster* lecherous swindler

---

70 *drôlesses* The Q1 reading falls between *drôles* (scoundrels) and *drôlesses*
(strumpets); the latter seems more likely.

RASOR
All! Ay, and a great deal too, I think.

MADAMOISELLE
Dou be fool, dou know noting. *Écoute, mon pauvre Rasor.*   80
Dou see des two eyes? Des two eyes have see de devil!

RASOR
The woman's mad.

MADAMOISELLE
In Spring Garden, dat rogue Constant meet dy lady—

RASOR
Bon!

MADAMOISELLE
I'll tell dee no more.   85

RASOR
Nay, prithee, my swan.

MADAMOISELLE (*Clapping her hands behind her, as he had done before*)
Come, kiss me den.

RASOR
I won't kiss you, not I.

MADAMOISELLE
Adieu!

RASOR
Hold! (*Gives her a hearty kiss*)—Now proceed.   90

MADAMOISELLE
Ah çà! I hide myself in one cunning place, where I hear all and see all. First, dy drunken master come *mal à propos*; but de sot no know his own dear wife, so he leave her to her sport. Den de game begin. (*As she speaks,* RASOR *still acts the man and she the woman*) De lover say soft ting; de lady look   95 upon de ground. He take her by de hand; she turn her head on oder way. Den he squeez very hard; den she pull—very softly. Den he take her in his arm; den she give him leetel pat. Den he kiss her *tétons*; den she say—pish! nay, fie! Den he tremble; den she—sigh. Den he pull her into de   100 arbour; den she pinch him.

RASOR
Ay, but not so hard, you baggage you.

80 *Écoute . . . Rasor* Listen, my dear Rasor
81 *Dou see* Q1–2 (Dou sees Q3, P)
84 *Bon!* Good!
91 *Ah çà!* Well then!
92 *mal à propos* unexpectedly
97 *on* Q2–3, P (one Q1)
99 *tétons* breasts

MADAMOISELLE

Den he grow bold; she grow weak. He tro her down, *il tombe dessus; le diable assiste, il emporte tout.* (RASOR *struggles with her, as if he would throw her down*)—Stand off, sirrah!   105

RASOR

You have set me afire, you jade you!

MADAMOISELLE

Den go to de river and quench dyself.

RASOR

What an unnatural harlot 'tis!

MADAMOISELLE (*Looking languishingly on him*)

Rasor.

RASOR

Madamoiselle?   110

MADAMOISELLE

Dou no love me?

RASOR

Not love thee?—More than a Frenchman does soup!

MADAMOISELLE

Den dou will refuse noting dat I bid dee?

RASOR

Don't bid me be damned then.

MADAMOISELLE

No; only tell dy master all I have tell dee of dy laty.   115

RASOR

Why, you little malicious strumpet, you! should you like to be served so?

MADAMOISELLE

Dou dispute den?—*Adieu!*

RASOR

Hold!—But why wilt thou make me be such a rogue, my dear?   120

MADAMOISELLE

Voilà un vrai Anglais! Il est amoureux, et cependant il veut raisonner. Va-t'en au diable!

RASOR

Hold once more. In hopes thou'lt give me up thy body, I resign thee up my soul.

103–4 *il ... tout* he falls on top of her; and with the devil's aid, carries all before him
109 s.d. *languishingly* Q1 (languishing Q2–3, P)
111 *me?* P (me Q1–3)
121–2 *Voilà ... diable!* There's a true Englishman! He's in love, and still he wants to argue. To the devil with you!

MADAMOISELLE
   Bon. Écoute donc: if dou fail me, I never see dee more; if dou   125
   obey me—(*She takes him about the neck, and gives him a*
   smacking kiss) *je m'abandonne à toi!*   (*Exit* MADAMOISELLE)
RASOR (*Licking his lips*)
   Not be a rogue?—*Amor vincit omnia!*   (*Exit* RASOR)

       Enter LADY FANCYFULL *and* MADAMOISELLE

LADY FANCYFULL
   Marry, say ye? Will the two things marry?
MADAMOISELLE
   On le va faire, matam.   130
LADY FANCYFULL
   Look you, Madamoiselle; in short, I can't bear it. No, I find
   I can't. If once I see 'em abed together, I shall have ten
   thousand thoughts in my head will make me run distracted.
   Therefore run and call Rasor back immediately, for some-
   thing must be done to stop this impertinent wedding. If I   135
   can but defer it four and twenty hours, I'll make such work
   about town with that little pert slut's reputation, he shall
   as soon marry a witch.
MADAMOISELLE (*Aside*)
   La voilà bien intentionnée!   (*Exeunt*)

Act V, Scene iv

CONSTANT's *Lodgings*
Enter CONSTANT *and* HEARTFREE

CONSTANT
   But what dost think will come of this business?
HEARTFREE
   'Tis easier to think what will not come on't.
CONSTANT
   What's that?

125 *Bon. Écoute donc* Good. Now listen
127 *je . . . toi!* I'm all yours!
128 *Amor vincit omnia!* Love conquers all! (proverbial)
130 *On . . . faire* They are arranging it
136 *but defer it* Q1 (defer it but Q2–3, P)
139 *La . . . intentionnée!* There's fine intentions!

---

132 *see 'em abed together* On the wedding night, it was usual for friends and
    relatives of the bride and groom to put them to bed, toss their stockings
    for luck, and serve them a sack-posset before withdrawing.

HEARTFREE

A challenge. I know the knight too well for that. His dear
body will always prevail upon his noble soul to be quiet.   5

CONSTANT

But though he dare not challenge me, perhaps he may
venture to challenge his wife.

HEARTFREE

Not if you whisper him in the ear, you won't have him do't;
and there's no other way left that I see. For as drunk as he
was, he'll remember you and I were where we should not   10
be; and I don't think him quite blockhead enough yet to
be persuaded we were got into his wife's closet only to peep
in her prayer-book.

Enter SERVANT, *with a letter*

SERVANT

Sir, here's a letter; a porter brought it.   [*Exit*]

CONSTANT

O ho, here's instructions for us.—(*Reads*) 'The accident that   15
has happened has touched our invention to the quick. We
would fain come off without your help, but find that's impossible. In a word, the whole business must be thrown upon
a matrimonial intrigue between your friend and mine. But if
the parties are not fond enough to go quite through with   20
the matter, 'tis sufficient for our turn they own the design.
We'll find pretences enough to break the match. Adieu'.—
Well, woman for invention! How long would my blockhead
have been a-producing this!—Hey, Heartfree! What, musing, man? Prithee be cheerful. What say'st thou, friend, to   25
this matrimonial remedy?

HEARTFREE

Why, I say it's worse than the disease.

CONSTANT

Here's a fellow for you! There's beauty and money on her
side, and love up to the ears on his; and yet—

HEARTFREE

And yet, I think I may reasonably be allowed to boggle at   30
marrying the niece, in the very moment that you are a-
debauching the aunt.

CONSTANT

Why truly, there may be something in that. But have not
you a good opinion enough of your own parts, to believe
you could keep a wife to yourself?   35

7 *challenge* bring a charge against
31–2 *a-debauching* Q1–3 (debauching P)

HEARTFREE

I should have, if I had a good opinion enough of hers, to believe she could do as much by me. For to do 'em right, after all, the wife seldom rambles till the husband shows her the way.

CONSTANT

'Tis true; a man of real worth scarce ever is a cuckold but by 40
his own fault. Women are not naturally lewd; there must be something to urge 'em to it. They'll cuckold a churl out of revenge, a fool because they despise him, a beast because they loathe him. But when they make bold with a man they once had a well-grounded value for, 'tis because they first 45
see themselves neglected by him.

HEARTFREE

Nay, were I well assured that I should never grow Sir John, I ne'er should fear Bellinda'd play my lady. But our weakness, thou know'st, my friend, consists in that very change we so impudently throw upon (indeed) a steadier and more 50
generous sex.

CONSTANT

Why faith, we are a little impudent in that matter; that's the truth on't. But this is wonderful, to see you grown so warm an advocate for those (but t'other day) you took so much pains to abuse! 55

HEARTFREE

All revolutions run into extremes: the bigot makes the boldest atheist, and the coyest saint the most extravagant strumpet. But, prithee, advise me in this good and evil, this life and death, this blessing and cursing, that is set before me. Shall I marry—or die a maid? 60

CONSTANT

Why faith, Heartfree, matrimony is like an army going to engage. Love's the forlorn hope, which is soon cut off; the marriage knot is the main body, which may stand buff a long, long time; and repentance is the rear-guard, which rarely gives ground as long as the main battle has a being. 65

HEARTFREE

Conclusion then: you advise me to whore on, as you do.

CONSTANT

That's not concluded yet. For though marriage be a lottery in which there are a wondrous many blanks, yet there is one inestimable lot in which the only heaven on earth is

62 *forlorn hope* vanguard which begins the attack
63 *stand buff* stand firm
65 *main battle* main body of troops

written. Would your kind fate but guide your hand to that,   70
though I were wrapped in all that luxury itself could clothe
me with, I still should envy you.

HEARTFREE
And justly, too; for to be capable of loving one, doubtless
is better than to possess a thousand. But how far that
capacity's in me, alas, I know not.   75

CONSTANT
But you would know?

HEARTFREE
I would so.

CONSTANT
Matrimony will inform you. Come, one flight of resolution
carries you to the land of experience; where, in a very
moderate time, you'll know the capacity of your soul and   80
your body both, or I'm mistaken.   (*Exeunt*)

Act V, Scene v

SIR JOHN BRUTE'*s House*
Enter LADY BRUTE *and* BELLINDA

BELLINDA
Well, madam, what answer have you from 'em?

LADY BRUTE
That they'll be here this moment. I fancy 'twill end in a
wedding: I'm sure he's a fool if it don't. Ten thousand
pound, and such a lass as you are, is no contemptible offer to
a younger brother. But are not you under strange agitations?   5
Prithee, how does your pulse beat?

BELLINDA
High and low; I have much ado to be valiant. Sure, it must
feel very strange to go to bed to a man.

LADY BRUTE
Um—it does feel a little odd at first, but it will soon grow
easy to you.   10

Enter CONSTANT *and* HEARTFREE

Good morrow, gentlemen. How have you slept after your
adventure?

HEARTFREE
Some careful thoughts, ladies, on your accounts have kept
us waking.

BELLINDA
And some careful thoughts on your own, I believe, have   15

7 *Sure, it must* P (*omitted* Q1–3)

hindered you from sleeping. Pray, how does this matrimonial project relish with you?

HEARTFREE

Why faith, e'en as storming towns does with soldiers, where the hope of delicious plunder banishes the fear of being knocked on the head.   20

BELLINDA

Is it then possible, after all, that you dare think of downright lawful wedlock?

HEARTFREE

Madam, you have made me so foolhardy I dare do anything.

BELLINDA

Then, sir, I challenge you; and matrimony's the spot where I expect you.   25

HEARTFREE

'Tis enough; I'll not fail.—(*Aside*) So, now I am in for Hobbes's voyage—a great leap in the dark.

LADY BRUTE

Well, gentlemen, this matter being concluded then, have you got your lessons ready? For Sir John is grown such an atheist of late, he'll believe nothing upon easy terms.   30

CONSTANT

We'll find ways to extend his faith, madam. But pray, how do you find him this morning?

LADY BRUTE

Most lamentably morose, chewing the cud after last night's discovery; of which however he had but a confused notion e'en now. But I'm afraid his *valet de chambre* has told him   35
all, for they are very busy together at this moment. When I told him of Bellinda's marriage, I had no other answer but a grunt; from which you may draw what conclusions you think fit.—But to your notes, gentlemen; he's here.

19 *hope* ed. (hopes Q1–3, P)   27 *Hobbes's* P (Hobs's Q1–2, Hob's Q3)
35 *his* Q1 (the Q2–3, P)   35 *valet de chambre* man-servant
39 *to your notes* 'i.e. to your parts in the arranged concert' (Dobrée); or perhaps another reference to the 'lessons' of 29

---

27 *leap . . . dark* 'a hazardous action undertaken in uncertainty as to the consequences' (*OED*). According to John Watkins, Thomas Hobbes said death was a leap in the dark (*Characteristic Anecdotes of Men of Learning and Genius* (1808), p. 276); following Heartfree, Vanbrugh applies the phrase to his own marriage in a letter dated 1 July 1719 (Dobrée, *Complete Works*, IV, 111).

39 s.d. *and* RASOR All four early editions bring on Rasor here, presumably on the strength of 36; but he has nothing to overhear until 101, and would be much better introduced ushering in the disguised Lady Fancyfull at 92.

Enter SIR JOHN *and* RASOR

CONSTANT

Good morrow, sir.   40

HEARTFREE

Good morrow, Sir John. I'm very sorry my indiscretion
should cause so much disorder in your family.

SIR JOHN

Disorders generally come from indiscretions, sir; 'tis no
strange thing at all.

LADY BRUTE

I hope, my dear, you are satisfied there was no wrong   45
intended you.

SIR JOHN

None, my dove.

BELLINDA

If not, I hope my consent to marry Mr Heartfree will convince you. For as little as I know of amours, sir, I can assure
you one intrigue is enough to bring four people together,   50
without further mischief.

SIR JOHN

And I know, too, that intrigues tend to procreation of more
kinds than one. One intrigue will beget another as soon as
beget a son or a daughter.

CONSTANT

I am very sorry, sir, to see you still seem unsatisfied with a   55
lady whose more than common virtue, I am sure, were she
my wife, should meet a better usage.

SIR JOHN

Sir, if her conduct has put a trick upon her virtue, her
virtue's the bubble, but her husband's the loser.

CONSTANT

Sir, you have received a sufficient answer already to justify   60
both her conduct and mine. You'll pardon me for meddling
in your family affairs; but I perceive I am the man you are
jealous of, and therefore it concerns me.

SIR JOHN

Would it did not concern me, and then I should not care
who it concerned.   65

CONSTANT

Well, sir, if truth and reason won't content you, I know

43   s.p. SIR JOHN ed. (*Constant* Q1–3, P)
52   *tend* Q2–3, P (tends Q1)
58   *put a trick upon* made a fool of
59   *bubble* (1) dupe (2) worthless delusion

but one way more which, if you think fit, you may take.

SIR JOHN

Lord, sir, you are very hasty! If I had been found at prayers
in your wife's closet, I should have allowed you twice as
much time to come to yourself in.   70

CONSTANT

Nay, sir, if time be all you want, we have no quarrel.

(SIR JOHN *muses*)

HEARTFREE [*To* CONSTANT, *aside*]

I told you how the sword would work upon him.

CONSTANT

Let him muse; however, I'll lay fifty pound our foreman
brings us in, not guilty.

SIR JOHN

(*Aside*) 'Tis well—'tis very well! In spite of that young   75
jade's matrimonial intrigue, I am a downright stinking
cuckold.—(*Putting his hand to his forehead*) Here they are.
Boo! Methinks I could butt with a bull.—What the plague
did I marry her for? I knew she did not like me; if she had,
she would have lain with me, for I would have done so   80
because I liked her. But that's past, and I have her.—And
now, what shall I do with her? If I put my horns in my
pocket, she'll grow insolent. If I don't, that goat there, that
stallion, is ready to whip me through the guts. The debate
then is reduced to this: shall I die a hero or live a rascal?—   85
Why, wiser men than I have long since concluded that a
living dog is better than a dead lion.—(*To* CONSTANT *and*
HEARTFREE) Gentlemen, now my wine and my passion are
governable, I must own I have never observed anything in
my wife's course of life to back me in my jealousy of her.   90
But jealousy's a mark of love; so she need not trouble her
head about it, as long as I make no more words on't.

LADY FANCYFULL *enters disguised, and addresses to* BELLINDA
apart

CONSTANT

I am glad to see your reason rule at last. Give me your hand;
I hope you'll look upon me as you are wont.

SIR JOHN

Your humble servant.—(*Aside*) A wheedling son of a whore!   95

HEARTFREE

And that I may be sure you are friends with me too, pray
give me your consent to wed your niece.

71 s.d. (SIR JOHN *muses*) Q1 prints this on the right of Heartfree's line
82 *in* Q1–3 (into P)

SIR JOHN
Sir, you have it with all my heart; damn me if you han't.—
(*Aside*) 'Tis time to get rid of her. A young, pert pimp!
she'll make an incomparable bawd in a little time.   100

Enter a SERVANT, *who gives* HEARTFREE *a letter.*

[*Exit* SERVANT]

BELLINDA
Heartfree your husband, say you? 'Tis impossible.
LADY FANCYFULL
Would to kind heaven it were! But 'tis too true; and in the
world there lives not such a wretch. I'm young; and either
I have been flattered by my friends, as well as glass, or
nature has been kind and generous to me. I had a fortune,   105
too, was greater far than he could ever hope for; but with
my heart I am robbed of all the rest. I'm slighted and I'm
beggared both at once. I have scarce a bare subsistence from
the villain, yet dare complain to none; for he has sworn if
e'er 'tis known I am his wife, he'll murder me. (*Weeping*)   110
BELLINDA
The traitor!
LADY FANCYFULL
I accidentally was told he courted you. Charity soon pre-
vailed upon me to prevent your misery; and, as you see,
I'm still so generous even to him, as not to suffer he should
do a thing for which the law might take away his life.   115
                                                        (*Weeping*)
BELLINDA [*Aside*]
Poor creature, how I pity her! (*They continue talking aside*)
HEARTFREE (*Aside*)
Death and damnation!—Let me read it again.—(*Reads*)
'Though I have a particular reason not to let you know who I
am till I see you, yet you'll easily believe 'tis a faithful
friend that gives you this advice. I have lain with Bellinda'.—   120
Good!—'I have a child by her'—Better and better!—'which
is now at nurse',—Heaven be praised!—'and I think the
foundation laid for another'.—Ha! Old truepenny!—'No
rack could have tortured this story from me; but friendship
has done it. I heard of your design to marry her, and could   125

123 *truepenny* trusty fellow (Zimansky sees an allusion to *Hamlet*, I.v.150, 161–2)

115 *law ... life* English law at this period treated bigamy as a felony punishable by death.

not see you abused. Make use of my advice, but keep my
secret till I ask you for't again. Adieu'.

(Exit LADY FANCYFULL)

CONSTANT (*To* BELLINDA)
Come, madam; shall we send for the parson? I doubt here's
no business for the lawyer; younger brothers have nothing
to settle but their hearts, and that I believe my friend here   130
has already done, very faithfully.

BELLINDA (*Scornfully*)
Are you sure, sir, there are no old mortgages upon it?

HEARTFREE (*Coldly*)
If you think there are, madam, it mayn't be amiss to defer
the marriage till you are sure they are paid off.

BELLINDA
(*Aside*) How the galled horse kicks!—(*To* HEARTFREE) We'll   135
defer it as long as you please, sir.

HEARTFREE
The more time we take to consider on't, madam, the less
apt we shall be to commit oversights; therefore, if you
please, we'll put it off for just nine months.

BELLINDA
Guilty consciences make men cowards; I don't wonder you   140
want time to resolve.

HEARTFREE
And they make women desperate; I don't wonder you were
so quickly determined.

BELLINDA
What does the fellow mean?

HEARTFREE
What does the lady mean?   145

SIR JOHN
Zoons, what do you both mean?

(HEARTFREE and BELLINDA walk chafing about)

RASOR (*Aside*)
Here is so much sport going to be spoiled, it makes me ready
to weep again. A pox o'this impertinent Lady Fancyfull and
her plots—and her Frenchwoman too! She's a whimsical,
ill-natured bitch; and when I have got my bones broke in   150
her service, 'tis ten to one but my recompense is a clap.—I
hear 'em tittering without still. Ecod, I'll e'en go lug 'em
both in by the ears and discover the plot, to secure my
pardon.   (*Exit* RASOR)

CONSTANT
Prithee explain, Heartfree.   155

HEARTFREE

A fair deliverance, thank my stars and my friend.

BELLINDA

'Tis well it went no farther. A base fellow!

LADY BRUTE

What can be the meaning of all this?

BELLINDA

What's his meaning, I don't know; but mine is, that if I
had married him—I had had no husband.   160

HEARTFREE

And what's her meaning, I don't know; but mine is, that
if I had married her—I had had wife enough.

SIR JOHN

Your people of wit have got such cramp ways of expressing
themselves, they seldom comprehend one another. Pox take
you both, will you speak that you may be understood?   165

Enter RASOR *in sackcloth, pulling in* LADY FANCYFULL *and*
MADAMOISELLE

RASOR

If they won't, here comes an interpreter.

LADY BRUTE

Heavens! What have we here?

PASOR

A villain—but a repenting villain. Stuff which saints in all
ages have been made of.

ALL

Rasor!   170

LADY BRUTE

What means this sudden metamorphose?

RASOR

Nothing, without my pardon.

LADY BRUTE

What pardon do you want?

RASOR

Imprimis, your ladyship's, for a damnable lie made upon your
spotless virtue and set to the tune of Spring Garden.—(*To*   175
SIR JOHN) Next, at my generous master's feet I bend, for
interrupting his more noble thoughts with phantoms
of disgraceful cuckoldom.—(*To* CONSTANT) Thirdly, I to
this gentleman apply, for making him the hero of my
romance.—(*To* HEARTFREE) Fourthly, your pardon, noble   180

163 *cramp* crabbed, indecipherable

sir, I ask, for clandestinely marrying you without either
bidding of banns, bishop's licence, friends' consent—or your
own knowledge.—(*To* BELLINDA) And lastly, to my good
young lady's clemency I come, for pretending the corn
was sowed in the ground before ever the plough had been   185
in the field.

SIR JOHN (*Aside*)
So that, after all, 'tis a moot point whether I am a cuckold
or not.

BELLINDA
Well sir, upon condition you confess all, I'll pardon you
myself, and try to obtain as much from the rest of the com-   190
pany. But I must know, then, who 'tis has put you upon all
this mischief.

RASOR
Satan and his equipage. Woman tempted me, lust weakened
me, and so the devil overcame me. As fell Adam, so fell I.

BELLINDA
Then pray, Mr Adam, will you make us acquainted with   195
your Eve?

RASOR (*To* MADAMOISELLE)
Unmask, for the honour of France.

ALL
Madamoiselle!

MADAMOISELLE
Me ask ten tousand pardon of all de good company.

SIR JOHN
Why, this mystery thickens instead of clearing up.—(*To*   200
RASOR) You son of a whore you, put us out of our pain.

RASOR
One moment brings sunshine.—(*Showing* MADAMOISELLE)
'Tis true, this is the woman that tempted me.—[*Pointing to*
LADY FANCYFULL] But this is the serpent that tempted the
woman; and if my prayers might be heard, her punishment   205
for so doing should be like the serpent's of old. (*Pulls off*
LADY FANCYFULL's *mask*) She should lie upon her face all
the days of her life.

ALL
Lady Fancyfull!

BELLINDA
Impertinent!   210

LADY BRUTE
Ridiculous!

ALL
Ha ha ha ha ha!

BELLINDA

I hope your ladyship will give me leave to wish you joy,
since you have owned your marriage yourself.—Mr Heart-
free, I vow 'twas strangely wicked in you to think of another   215
wife, when you had one already so charming as her ladyship.

ALL

Ha ha ha ha ha!

LADY FANCYFULL (*Aside*)

Confusion seize 'em, as it seizes me!

MADAMOISELLE [*Aside*]

Que le diable étouffe ce maraud de Rasor!

BELLINDA

Your ladyship seems disordered. A breeding qualm, perhaps?   220
Mr Heartfree, your bottle of Hungary water to your lady!—
Why, madam, he stands as unconcerned as if he were your
husband in earnest.

LADY FANCYFULL

Your mirth's as nauseous as yourself, Bellinda. You think
you triumph o'er a rival now. *Hélas, ma pauvre fille!*   225
Where'er I'm rival there's no cause for mirth. No, my poor
wretch; 'tis from another principle I have acted. I knew that
thing there would make so perverse a husband, and you so
impertinent a wife, that lest your mutual plagues should
make you both run mad, I charitably would have broke the   230
match. He he he he he!

  (*Exit laughing affectedly*, MADAMOISELLE *following her*)

MADAMOISELLE

He he he he he!

ALL

Ha ha ha ha ha!

SIR JOHN (*Aside*)

Why, now this woman will be married to somebody too.

BELLINDA

Poor creature, what a passion she's in! But I forgive her.   235

HEARTFREE

Since you have so much goodness for her, I hope you'll
pardon my offence too, madam.

219 *étouffe* ed. (e toute Q1–3, P)
219 *Que . . . Rasor!* May the devil choke that scoundrel Rasor!
221 *Hungary* P (Hungry Q1–3)
225 *o'er* Q1–3 (over P)
225 *Hélas . . . fille!* Alas, my poor girl!

---

221 *Hungary water* a restorative distilled from rosemary flowers, and
  'denominated from a Queen of *Hungary*, for whose Use it was first
  prepar'd' (Ephraim Chambers, *Cyclopaedia* (1728), I, 263)

BELLINDA

There will be no great difficulty in that, since I am guilty of an equal fault.

HEARTFREE

Then pardons being passed on all sides, pray let's to church   240
to conclude the day's work.

CONSTANT

But before you go, let me treat you, pray, with a song a new-married lady made within this week; it may be of use to you both.

SONG

I

When yielding first to Damon's flame   245
    I sunk into his arms,
He swore he'd ever be the same,
    Then rifled all my charms.
But fond of what he'd long desired,
    Too greedy of his prey,   250
My shepherd's flame, alas, expired
    Before the verge of day.

II

My innocence in lovers' wars
    Reproached his quick defeat;
Confused, ashamed, and bathed in tears,   255
    I mourned his cold retreat.
At length, 'Ah, shepherdess', cried he,
    'Would you my fire renew,
Alas, you must retreat like me;
    I'm lost if you pursue'.   260

HEARTFREE

So, madam; now had the parson but done his business—

BELLINDA

You'd be half weary of your bargain.

HEARTFREE

No, sure, I might dispense with one night's lodging.

BELLINDA

I'm ready to try, sir.

HEARTFREE

Then let's to church.   265
    And if it be our chance to disagree—

BELLINDA

    Take heed—the surly husband's fate you see.

FINIS

249 *he'd* ed. (h'ad Q1–3, P)   263 *dispense with* tolerate

EPILOGUE
By another hand
Spoken by LADY BRUTE *and* BELLINDA

LADY BRUTE
No epilogue?
BELLINDA   I swear I know of none.
LADY BRUTE
Lord! How shall we excuse it to the town?
BELLINDA
Why, we must e'en say something of our own.
LADY BRUTE
Our own! Ay, that must needs be precious stuff.
BELLINDA
I'll lay my life, they'll like it well enough.   5
Come, faith, begin—
LADY BRUTE   Excuse me, after you.
BELLINDA
Nay, pardon me for that; I know my cue.
LADY BRUTE
Oh, for the world, I would not have precedence.
BELLINDA
O Lord!
LADY BRUTE I swear—
BELLINDA   O fie!
LADY BRUTE   I'm all obedience.
First then, know all, before our doom is fixed,   10
The third day is for us—
BELLINDA   Nay, and the sixt.
LADY BRUTE
We speak not from the poet now, nor is it
His cause—(I want a rhyme)—
BELLINDA   That we solicit.
LADY BRUTE
Then, sure, you cannot have the hearts to be severe
And damn us—
BELLINDA   Damn us! Let 'em if they dare.   15

Epilogue Q1 prints this immediately after the Prologue
11 *sixt* Q1 (sixth Q2–3, P)

---

11 The profits of the third, sixth, and ninth performances went to the
dramatist; Vanbrugh has donated his to the actors.

LADY BRUTE

Why, if they should, what punishment remains?

BELLINDA

Eternal exile from behind our scenes.

LADY BRUTE

But if they're kind, that sentence we'll recall;
We can be grateful—

BELLINDA   And have wherewithal.

LADY BRUTE

But at grand treaties hope not to be trusted,   20
Before preliminaries are adjusted.

BELLINDA

You know the time, and we appoint this place;
Where, if you please, we'll meet and sign the peace.

---

17 Despite many prohibitions from the Lord Chamberlain, gallants
frequently went visiting backstage during the performance.

20-3 Another reference to Ryswick, where preliminaries were adjusted
throughout the summer and the peace finally signed in September 1697.

Appendix A

THE REVISED SCENES

THESE SCENES, IN which Sir John attacks the law dressed in his wife's gown instead of the parson's, were first published in a Dublin edition of 1743; the title-page reads: 'THE Provok'd Wife: A COMEDY. In which is inserted, an Original SCENE, never before printed'. There were two issues, one printed by Edw. Bate for James Kelburn, the other by S. Powell for George Risk. The first London printing was in an appendix to the play in the first volume of Vanbrugh's *Plays* (1759); most later editions simply substituted them for the original scenes. I have taken as my copy-text the Bodleian Library copy of the Risk issue of the 1743 edition (Vet A4.f.1198), collated against the British Museum copy of 1759 (11771.d.8). As *1759* (L) is not dependent upon *1743* (D), I have thought it worth while to gloss all significant variants.

The new scenes were probably written to remove from the play that strain of clerical satire which had so antagonized Collier and his moralizing friends in the Society for the Reformation of Manners:

> Sir *John Brute* puts on the Habit of a Clergyman, counterfeits himself drunk; quarrels with the *Constable*, and is knock'd down and seiz'd. He rails, swears, curses, is lewd and profane, to all the Heights of Madness and Debauchery: The *Officers* and *Justice* break jests upon him, and make him a sort of Representative of his *Order*. This is rare *Protestant* Diversion, and very much for the Credit of the *Reformation*![1]

—a charge to which Vanbrugh had replied very smartly in his *Short Vindication* of 1698.

It is not known when these revised scenes were first performed, for during Vanbrugh's lifetime the play was advertised with alterations on three separate occasions. The first was at the Queen's Theatre on 19 January 1706, when Vanbrugh as manager of the theatre was busy trying to fill it by revising his own earlier work. *Squire Trelooby*, which he had originally adapted from Molière in conjunction with Walsh and Congreve, was announced for 28 January 1706 with 'the last Act being entirely new';[2] and Trelooby also parades before the constable and watch dressed as a lady of

[1] Jeremy Collier, *A Short View of the Immorality and Profaneness of the English Stage* (1698), p. 108.
[2] *The London Stage 1660–1800*, ed. W. Van Lennep, E. L. Avery, A. H. Scouten, G. Winchester Stone Jnr, and C. B. Hogan (Carbondale, Illinois, 1960–68), Pt. 2, 115; see also John B. Shipley, 'The authorship of *The Cornish Squire*', *Philological Quarterly*, XLVII (1968), 147.

quality. This parallel with Sir John is strong evidence that the revised scenes were *not* performed at this time, for who would pay to see Trelooby *en travesti* if he had seen Sir John as Lady Brute at the same theatre only ten days before? The 'Alterations' of 1706, like the phrase 'Carefully Revis'd' in the playbills at Lincoln's Inn Fields for 21 December 1715,[3] probably meant no more than the addition of a new song or two, the revision of some outdated topical references to Ryswick and the Bank of England, and the deletion of those 'profane' lines for which Betterton's company had been prosecuted in 1701.[4] There is more convincing evidence for the revival staged at Drury Lane on 11 January 1726. Firstly, the advertisement reads: 'Never Acted there before. Revis'd by the Author'.[5] This is the first time the revisions are directly attributed to Vanbrugh; and Vanbrugh, who was in London in December 1725 and again in March 1726, is not known to have contradicted them. Secondly, they are supported by the independent testimony of Colley Cibber:

> In 1725 we were call'd upon, in a manner that could not be resisted, to revive the *Provok'd Wife*, a Comedy which, while we found our Account in keeping the Stage clear of those loose Liberties it had formerly too justly been charg'd with, we had laid aside for some Years. The Author, Sir *John Vanbrugh*, who was conscious of what it had too much of, was prevail'd upon to substitute a new-written Scene in the Place of one in the fourth Act, where the Wantonness of his Wit and Humour had (originally) made a Rake talk like a Rake in the borrow'd Habit of a Clergyman: To avoid which Offence, he clapt the same Debauchee into the Undress of a Woman of Quality: Now the Character and Profession of a Fine Lady not being so indelibly sacred as that of a Churchman, whatever Follies he expos'd in the Petticoat kept him at least clear of his former Prophaneness, and were now innocently ridiculous to the Spectator.[6]

Cibber played Brute in the Drury Lane revival; his evidence is unambiguous, and he was surely in a position to know the truth. The only difficulty arises from Harper's song (printed in Appendix B), which clearly describes Sir John in his parson's gown. It was published in 1729, and between 15 September 1726 and 16 October 1729 Harper is known to have played Colonel Bully at Drury Lane on at least five separate occasions. Of course, the song may date from 1719–21, when Harper was with Quin at Lincoln's Inn Fields and presumably still playing the Hiccup scenes. But if it dates from

[3] *The London Stage*, Pt. 2, 115 and 381.
[4] See J. W. Krutch, *Comedy and Conscience after the Restoration* (New York, 1924), pp. 169–73.
[5] *The London Stage*, Pt. 2, 850.
[6] Colley Cibber, *An Apology for the Life of Mr Colley Cibber*, ed. R. W. Lowe (1889), II, 233–4.

his later engagement at Drury Lane, as seems more likely, it suggests that Cibber reverted to the original scenes when the novelty of the revised ones had been exhausted. Such a change may well date from 9 November 1727, when the Drury Lane playbills first dropped 'Revis'd by the Author' in favour of 'Written by the late Sir John Vanbrugh'. [7]

In any event, during the 1730s the new scenes became common property. Bridgwater played them at Covent Garden on 22 March 1735, and Quin (now at Drury Lane) took them up on 23 April, advertising 'the Scene in Women's Cloaths' as if it were a novelty.[8] Garrick revelled in them, revealing an acute observation of

> the many various Airs of the Fair Sex: He is perfectly versed in the Exercise of the Fan, the Lips, the Adjustment of the Tucker, and even the minutest Conduct of the Finger.[9]

A painting by Zoffany shows him attacking the watch in 'a yellow satin brocaded dress with a white lining, a green lace shawl and a lace cap with pink ribbons', and for his last season he wore a ridiculous bonnet decorated with ribbons, feathers, oranges and lemons, and a bouquet or two of flowers.[10] Most modern Brutes have played the revised scenes. Mervyn Johns in 1936 and Russell Waters in 1950 both made them 'irresistibly funny', and one critic found Trevor Martin's portrayal of a 'pathological woman-hater' dressed up in his wife's clothes 'psychologically revealing as well as extremely funny'.[11] These tributes are well justified. The revised scenes add a fresh dimension to the role of Sir John Brute, and afford almost limitless opportunities for the kind of transvestite farce associated with *Charley's Aunt*. They also have far greater dramatic relevance than the Hiccup scenes. Sir John's satiric account of the life of a lady of fashion reflects back upon the empty vanities of Lady Fancyfull, while his grotesque and implausible impersonation of Lady Brute keeps the contrasting character of the real Lady Brute always in our mind. Even in disguise, however, Sir John retains his own character; his 'Lady Brute' is nothing more than the feminine version of himself, a gambling lady rake bent like him upon ruining her marriage by a career of selfish debauchery. Vanbrugh presents her more fully as Lady Arabella Loverule in his unfinished masterpiece *A Journey to London*; here, she gives depth

[7] *The London Stage*, Pt. 2, 943.

[8] *The London Stage*, Pt. 3, 482.

[9] The *London Chronicle*, 3–5 March 1757, quoted in K. A. Burnim, *David Garrick, Director* (Pittsburgh, 1961), pp. 183–4.

[10] See Burnim, p. 184; Zoffany's painting is described in R. Mander and J. Mitchenson, *The Artist and the Theatre* (1955), p. 49.

[11] *The Times*, 6 October 1936; *The Times*, 23 March 1950; the *Observer*, 28 July 1963.

to the farce. For in the ironic interplay between Sir John, Lady
Brute, and Sir John's 'Lady Brute' Vanbrugh provides a cool and
unexpected commentary upon those matrimonial problems which
form the core of his play.

Act IV, Scene i

Covent Garden
Enter LORD RAKE, SIR JOHN, [COLONEL BULLY] *&c., with*
swords drawn

LORD RAKE
   Is the dog dead?
COLONEL BULLY
   No, damn him, I heard him wheeze.
LORD RAKE
   How the witch his wife howled!
COLONEL BULLY
   Ay, she'll alarm the watch presently.
LORD RAKE
   Appear, knight, then; come, you have a good cause to fight   5
   for: there's a man murdered.
SIR JOHN
   Is there? Then let his ghost be satisfied; for I'll sacrifice a
   constable to it presently, and burn his body upon his wooden
   chair.

Enter a TAILOR, *with a bundle under his arm*

COLONEL BULLY
   How now! What have we got here, a thief?   10
TAILOR
   No, an't please you; I'm no thief.
LORD RAKE
   That we'll see presently.—Here, let the general examine him.
SIR JOHN
   Ay, ay; let me examine him, and I'll lay a hundred pound I
   find him guilty in spite of his teeth—for he looks—like a—
   sneaking rascal.—Come sirrah, without equivocation or   15
   mental reservation, tell me of what opinion you are and
   what calling; for by them—I shall guess at your morals.
TAILOR
   An't please you, I'm a dissenting journeyman woman's
   tailor.
SIR JOHN
   Then, sirrah, you love lying by your religion and theft by   20
18–19 *woman's tailor* L (tailor D)

your trade. And so, that your punishment may be suitable
to your crimes, I'll have you first gagged—and then hanged.

TAILOR

Pray, good worthy gentlemen, don't abuse me; indeed I'm
an honest man, and a good workman, though I say it that
should not say it. 25

SIR JOHN

No words, sirrah, but attend your fate.

LORD RAKE

Let me see what's in that bundle.

TAILOR

An't please you, it is my lady's short cloak and wrapping-
gown.

SIR JOHN

What lady, you reptile you? 30

TAILOR

My Lady Brute, your honour.

SIR JOHN

My Lady Brute! My wife! The robe of my wife—with
reverence let me approach it! The dear angel is always taking
care of me in danger, and has sent me this suit of armour to
protect me in this day of battle. On they go! 35

ALL

O brave knight!

LORD RAKE

Live Don Quixote the Second!

SIR JOHN

Sancho, my squire, help me on with my armour.

TAILOR

O dear gentlemen, I shall be quite undone if you take the
gown. 40

SIR JOHN

Retire, sirrah; and since you carry off your skin—go home,
and be happy.

TAILOR

I think I'd e'en as good follow the gentleman's advice, for
if I dispute any longer, who knows but the whim may take
'em to case me? These courtiers are fuller of tricks than they 45
are of money; they'll sooner break a man's bones than pay
his bill. (*Exit*)

28 *it is* D (it's L)
28–9 *wrapping-gown* D (sack L) night-gown
31 *Brute, your* D (Brute, an't please your L)
36 s.p. ALL L (Om. D)
40 *gown* D (sack L)

SIR JOHN
So, how d'ye like my shapes now?
LORD RAKE
To a miracle! He looks like a queen of the Amazons.—But
to your arms, gentlemen! The enemy's upon their march;   50
here's the watch.
SIR JOHN
Oons, if it were Alexander the Great at the head of his army,
I would drive him into a horse-pond.
ALL
Huzza! O brave knight!

Enter WATCHMEN

SIR JOHN
See, here he comes with all his Greeks about him.—Follow   55
me, boys!
1 WATCHMAN
Hey-day! Who have we got here? Stand!
SIR JOHN
Mayhap not!
1 WATCHMAN
What are you all doing here in the street at this time of
night? And who are you, madam, that seem to be at the head   60
of this noble crew?
SIR JOHN
Sirrah, I am Bonduca, Queen of the Welshmen; and with a
leek as long as my pedigree I will destroy your Roman
legion in an instant.—Britons, strike home!

48 *d'ye* L (do you D)
54 s.p. ALL L (Om. D)
54 s.d. L. D prints this after Sir John's next line
55 *Greeks* sharpers, rogues
58 *Mayhap* perhaps
59 *street* D (streets L)
59–60 *of night* D (o'night L)

---

62 *Bonduca* warrior-queen of the Iceni in Fletcher's tragedy *Bonduca*
(1613?), revived with music by Purcell in 1695. 'Britons, strike home'
is sung by the Druids in III.ii of the adaptation:
    To Arms, to Arms: Your Ensigns strait display:
    Now, now, now, set the Battle in Array. . . .
Britains, *Strike Home: Revenge your Country's Wrongs:*
Fight and Record your selves in Druids *Songs.*
                                         (*Bonduca* (1696), p. 22).
63 *leek . . . pedigree* Vanbrugh pokes fun at the Welsh fondness for tracing
pedigrees in *I Aesop*, III.i.42–63.

(They fight off. WATCHMEN *return with* SIR JOHN)

1 WATCHMAN

So! We have got the queen, however. We'll make her pay   65
well for her ransom.—Come, madam, will your majesty
please to walk before the constable?

SIR JOHN

The constable's a rascal! And you are a son of a whore!

1 WATCHMAN

A most princely reply, truly! If this be her royal style, I'll
warrant her maids of honour prattle prettily; but we'll teach   70
you a little of our court dialect before we part with you,
princess.—Away with her to the round-house.

SIR JOHN

Hands off, you ruffians! My honour's dearer to me than
my life! I hope you won't be uncivil.

1 WATCHMAN

Away with her!   75

SIR JOHN

Oh, my honour! my honour!   *(Exeunt)*

Act IV, Scene iii

A Street

Enter CONSTABLE *and* WATCHMEN, *with* SIR JOHN

CONSTABLE

Come, forsooth; come along, if you please! I once in compassion thought to have seen you safe home this morning;
but you have been so rampant and abusive all night, I shall
see what the justice of peace will say to you.

SIR JOHN

And you shall see what I'll say to the justice of peace.   5

(WATCHMAN knocks at the door)

Enter SERVANT

CONSTABLE

Is Mr Justice at home?

SERVANT

Yes.

CONSTABLE

Pray acquaint his worship, we have got an unruly woman

64 s.d. L (*Fights* D)
65 *queen* punning on *quean*, 'a bold, impudent, or ill-behaved woman' (*OED*)
69 *princely* D (noble L)   71 *a little* D (some L)
76 D; *omitted in* L
    s.d. *A Street* L (Like Q1, D does not begin a new scene here)
5   s.d. L (Watch *knocks, a* Servant *enters* D)

here, and desire to know what he'll please to have done with
her.   10

SERVANT

I'll acquaint my master.   (*Exit*)

SIR JOHN

Hark you, constable, what cuckoldly justice is this?

CONSTABLE

One that will know how to deal with such romps as you are,
I'll warrant you.

Enter JUSTICE

JUSTICE

Well, Mr Constable, what's the matter here?   15

CONSTABLE

An't please your worship, this here comical sort of a gentlewoman has committed great outrages tonight. She has been
frolicking with my Lord Rake and his gang; they attacked
the watch, and I hear there has been a gentleman killed.
I believe 'tis they have done it.   20

SIR JOHN

There may have been murder, for aught I know; and 'tis a
great mercy there has not been a rape too—for this fellow
would have ravished me.

1 WATCHMAN

Ravish! I ravish! O lud, O lud, O lud! I ravish her? Why,
please your honour, I heard Mr Constable say he believed   25
she was little better than a mophrodite.

JUSTICE

Why truly, she does seem to be a little masculine about the
mouth.

1 WATCHMAN

Yes, and about the hands too, an't please your worship. I
did but offer in mere civility to help her up the steps into 30

13 *will know* D (knows L)
13 *romps* boisterous women
15 *what's* D (what is L)
17 *tonight* last night (also at 57)
19 *gentleman* D (man L)
20 *done it* L (done't D)
21 *There* D (Sir, there L)
22 *for this* D (that L)
24 *Ravish! I ravish!* D (Ravish! Ravish! L)
24 *I ravish her?* D (Ravish her! L)
25 *honour* D (worship L)
26 *mophrodite* D (maphrodite L) vulgar corruption of *hermaphrodite*
27 *to be a* D (a L)

our apartment, and with her gripen fist—(SIR JOHN *knocks him down*)—ay, just so, sir.

SIR JOHN
I felled him to the ground like an ox.

JUSTICE
Out upon this boisterous woman! Out upon her!

SIR JOHN
Mr Justice, he would have been uncivil. It was in defence   35
of my honour, and I demand satisfaction.

1 WATCHMAN
I hope your worship will satisfy her honour in Bridewell;
that fist of hers will make an admirable hemp-beater.

SIR JOHN
Sir, I hope you will protect me against that libidinous
rascal; I am a woman of quality, and virtue too, for all I am   40
in a sort of an undress this morning.

JUSTICE
Why, she really has the air of a sort of a woman a little
somethingish out of the common.—Madam, if you expect
I should be favourable to you, I desire I may know who
you are.   45

SIR JOHN
Sir, I am anybody, at your service.

JUSTICE
Lady, I desire to know your name.

SIR JOHN
Sir, my name's Mary.

JUSTICE
Ay, but your surname, madam?

SIR JOHN
Sir, my surname's the very same with my husband's.   50

JUSTICE
A strange woman this!—Who is your husband, pray?

SIR JOHN
Why, Sir John.

JUSTICE
Sir John who?

31 *gripen* L (gippen D) clenched
31–2 s.d. D and L print this at the end of the Watchman's speech
41 *a sort of an* D (an L)
42 *really has* D (has really L)
43 *somethingish* D (something L)
52 *Why, Sir* D (Sir L)

37 *Bridewell* a house of correction near Fleet Street, where night-walkers
and other petty offenders were set to hard labour pounding hemp

SIR JOHN
Why, Sir John Brute.
JUSTICE
Is it possible, madam, you can be my Lady Brute?   55
SIR JOHN
That happy woman, sir, am I; only a little in my merriment tonight.
JUSTICE
I'm concerned for Sir John.
SIR JOHN
Truly, so am I.
JUSTICE
I've heard he's an honest gentleman.   60
SIR JOHN
As ever drank.
JUSTICE
Good lack! Indeed, lady, I am sorry he should have such a wife.
SIR JOHN
Sir, I am sorry he has any wife at all.
JUSTICE
And so, perhaps, may he.—I doubt you have not given him   65
a very good taste of matrimony.
SIR JOHN
Taste, sir? I have scorned to stint him to a taste; I have given him a full meal of it.
JUSTICE
Indeed, I believe so!—But pray, fair lady, may he have given you any occasion for this extraordinary conduct?   70
Does he not use you well?
SIR JOHN
A little upon the rough, sometimes.
JUSTICE
Ay, any man may be out of humour now and then.
SIR JOHN
Sir, I love peace and quiet, and when a woman don't find

54 *Why, Sir* D (Sir L)
58 *I'm* D (I am L)
60 *I've* D (I have L)
62 *I am* D (I'm L)
62 *should have* D (has L)
64 s.p. SIR JOHN L (*Justice* D)
64 *Sir, I* D (I L)
67 *I have scorned* D (Sir, I have scorned L)
72 *upon the rough* harshly

that at home, she's apt sometimes to comfort herself with a   75
few innocent diversions abroad.

JUSTICE

I doubt he uses you but too well. Pray, how does he as to
that weighty thing, money? Does he allow you what's proper
of that?

SIR JOHN

Sir, I have generally enough to pay the reckoning, if this   80
son of a whore the drawer would bring his bill.

JUSTICE

A strange woman this.—Does he spend a reasonable portion
of his time at home, to the comfort of his wife and children?

SIR JOHN

Never gave his wife cause to repine at his being abroad in
his life.   85

JUSTICE

Pray, madam, how may he be in the grand matrimonial
point: is he true to your bed?

SIR JOHN

Chaste?—Oons, this fellow asks so many impertinent
questions, egad, I believe it is the justice's wife in the
justice's clothes.   90

JUSTICE

'Tis a great pity he should have been thus disposed of.—
Pray, madam, and then I have done, what may be your
ladyship's common method of life, if I may presume so far?

SIR JOHN

Why, sir, much like that of a woman of quality.

JUSTICE

Pray how may you generally pass your time, madam? Your   95
morning, for example?

SIR JOHN

Sir, like a woman of quality. I wake about two o'clock in the
afternoon, I stretch, and then—make a sign for my choco-
late. When I have drank three cups, I slide down again upon
my back, with my arms over my head, while two maids put   100

78 *what's* D (what is L)
81 *the drawer* D (of a drawer L)
81 *bring* D (but bring L)
84 *Never* D (He never L)
92 *I have* D (I've L)
94 *much like* D (much L)
98 *and then* D (and L)
100 *two* D (my two L)
100 *put* L (puts D)

on my stockings. Then, hanging upon their shoulders, I am
trailed to my great chair, where I sit, and yawn for my
breakfast. If it don't come presently, I lie down upon my
couch to say my prayers, while my maid reads me the
playbills.   105
JUSTICE
Very well, madam.
SIR JOHN
When the tea is brought in, I drink twelve regular dishes,
with eight slices of bread and butter—and half an hour
after, I send to the cook to know if the dinner is almost ready.
JUSTICE
So, madam.   110
SIR JOHN
By that time my head's half-dressed, I hear my husband
swearing himself into a state of perdition that the meat's all
cold upon the table; to mend which, I come down in an
hour more and have it sent back to the kitchen to be all
dressed over again.   115
JUSTICE
Poor man!
SIR JOHN
When I have dined, and my idle servants are presumptuously
set down at their ease to do so too, I call for my coach, go
to visit fifty dear friends, of whom I hope I never shall find
one at home while I shall live.   120
JUSTICE
So; there's the morning and afternoon pretty well disposed
of.—Pray, madam, how do you pass your evenings?
SIR JOHN
Like a woman of spirit, sir, a great spirit. Give me a box
and dice—seven's the main! Oons, sir, I set you a hundred

111 *head's* D (head is L)
113 *mend* D (amend L)
118–19 *go to visit* D (to go visit L)
119 *never shall* D (shall never L)
124 *set* stake

---

105 *playbills* regularly delivered to the town houses of wealthy patrons of
   the theatre
111 *head's half-dressed* The lofty head-dresses affected by ladies of fashion,
   which took several hours to erect, are ridiculed in the *Spectator*, no. 98,
   22 June 1711.
124 *seven's the main* In the game of hazard, the 'main' is a number between
   five and nine called by the caster before the dice are thrown; the odds
   against casting seven on any particular throw are five to one.

pounds! Why, do you think women are married now-a-days   125
to sit at home and mend napkins? Sir, we have nobler ways
of passing time.

JUSTICE

Mercy upon us, Mr Constable, what will this age come to?

CONSTABLE

What will it come to, indeed, if such women as these are
not set in the stocks?   130

SIR JOHN

I have a little urgent business calls upon me; and therefore
I desire the favour of you to bring matters to a conclusion.

JUSTICE

Madam, if I were sure that business were not to commit
more disorders, I would release you.

SIR JOHN

None—by my virtue!   135

JUSTICE

Then, Mr Constable, you may discharge her.

SIR JOHN

Sir, your very humble servant. If you please to accept of a
bottle—

JUSTICE

I thank you kindly, madam; but I never drink in a morning.
Good-bye, madam, good-bye to ye.   140

SIR JOHN

Good-bye t'ye, good sir. (*Exit* JUSTICE) So.—Now, Mr
Constable, shall you and I go pick up a whore together?

CONSTABLE

No, thank you, madam; my wife's enough to satisfy any
reasonable man.

SIR JOHN

(*Aside*) He he he he he! The fool is married then.—[*Aloud*] 145
Well, you won't go?

CONSTABLE

Not I, truly.

SIR JOHN

Then I'll go by myself; and you and your wife may be
damned.   (*Exit* SIR JOHN)

CONSTABLE (*Gazing after him*)

Why, God a mercy, my lady!   (*Exeunt*)   150

125 *pounds* D (pound L)
131 *I have* D (Sir, I have L)
150 s.d. *him* D (her L)
150 *my lady* D (lady L)

Appendix B

TWO ADDITIONAL SONGS

I

Vanbrugh's songs for the play were soon replaced by others on the stage, and as Treble and Pipe withdrew from the cast lists new singers arrived to provide music at different places in the text. Mrs Willis, who played Madamoiselle, sang the 'Ballad of Sally' at Lincoln's Inn Fields on 20 April 1719, and on 19 March 1726 the same theatre announced 'new Songs proper to the Play, compos'd and sung by Leveridge and Legare'.[1] Since Colonel Bully has only seven lines, his role was an obvious one for a singer who could also act. John Beard, for whom Handel wrote some of his finest tenor parts, played it on 8 January 1742 at Drury Lane, where his predecessor John Harper probably sang the following ditty some time between 15 September 1726 and 16 October 1729. (The problems involved here are discussed in the introduction to Appendix A.) There is no obvious place for this song in Vanbrugh's text, but it would go well at the end of IV.i, when Bully could make a cautious reappearance as the watch go off.

The song was printed in *The Musical Miscellany; Being a Collection of Choice Songs, Set to the Violin and Flute, By the most Eminent Masters* (1729), I, 66–8, which also prints the tenor line. My copytext is the Bodleian Library copy (Douce M.601).[2]

TIPPLING JOHN
Sung by Mr Harper, in *The Provoked Wife*

As tippling John was jogging on,
    Upon the riot night,
With tottering pace and fiery face,
    Suspicious of high flight,
The guards who took him, by his look,   5
    For some chief firebrand,
Asked whence he came, what was his name,
    'Who are you? Stand, friend, stand!'

[1] *The London Stage 1660–1800*, ed. W. Van Lennep, E. L. Avery, A. H. Scouten, G. Winchester Stone Jnr, and C. B. Hogan (Carbondale, Illinois, 1960–68), Pt. 2, 536 and 859.
[2] I owe my knowledge of this song to Frank M. Patterson, 'The revised scenes of *The Provok'd Wife*,' *English Language Notes*, IV (1966–67), 19–23, which raises matters discussed in the introduction to Appendix A.

'I'm going home, from meeting come'.
 'Ay', says one, 'that's the case;   10
Some meeting he has burnt, you see,
 The flame's still in his face'.
John thought 'twas time to purge the crime,
 And said 'twas his intent
For to assuage his thirsty rage;   15
 That meeting 'twas he meant.

'Come, friend, be plain; you trifle in vain',
 Says one, 'pray let us know,
That we may find how you're inclined,
 Are you high church or low?'   20
John said to that, 'I'll tell you what,
 To end debates and strife,
All I can say, this is the way
 I steer my course of life:

I ne'er to Bow, nor Burgess go,   25
 To steeple-house nor hall;
The brisk bar-bell best suits my zeal
 With "Gentlemen, d'ye call?"
Now judge, am I low church or high,
 From tavern or the steeple,   30
Whose merry toll exalts the soul
 And makes us high-flown people'.

The guards came on and looked at John
 With countenance most pleasant;
By whisper round they all soon found   35
 He was no dangerous peasant.
So while John stood the best he could,
 Expecting their decision,
'Pox on't!' says one, 'let him be gone,
 He's of our own religion'.   40

---

 9 *meeting* (1) private party (2) nonconformist gathering
11 *burnt* fired with zeal
25 *Bow* probably St Mary-le-Bow, Cheapside
25 *Burgess* town hall (not in *OED*)
26 *steeple-house* term used by Quakers for *church*
32 *high-flown* (1) intoxicated (2) extremist for church authority
38 *Expecting* awaiting

II

This Scottish medley, which seems to have two distinct choruses and is sometimes printed without the second stanza, marks that moment in the stage history of *The Provoked Wife* when Colonel Bully's success as a singer enabled him to steal even the tavern scene from Lord Rake. It was first printed in the 1776 edition of the play, immediately after 'What a pother of late' with the comment: 'Instead of this song by Lord *Rake*, the following by Colonel *Bully* is now sung at the Theatre'. This probably refers to the performances that season at Drury Lane, where a contemporary witness shows it brought the house down on 30 April 1776,

> Being the last time of Garrick's appearing in character of Sir John Brute. When the Song Encor'd Mr Garrick said Come Col. give us that Song again for two very good Reasons, the first because your friends desire it—and Secondly because I believe I shall never be in such good company again.[3]

I have taken as my copy-text the Bodleian Library copy of *1776* (Vet A5.e.4335), collated against the British Museum copy of the text in an undated broadside entitled 'A Scotch Medley. *Introduced in The Provok'd Wife*' (11621.i.11). The broadside (SM) generally makes better sense of the dialect than *1776* (L).

SONG by COLONEL BULLY

We're gaily yet, and we're gaily yet,
And we's no very fou, but we're gaily yet.
Then sit ye awhile, and tipple a bit,
For we's no very fou, but we're gaily yet.

There was a lad, and they cau'd him Dicky,   5
He gae me a kiss, and I bit his lippy,
Then under my apron he showed me a trick.
And we's no very fou, but we're gaily yet.
    And we're gaily yet, &c.

There were three lads and they were clad,   10
There were three lasses and them they had.
Three trees in the orchard are newly sprung,

2 *we's* L (we're SM)
2 *no* SM (not L)
2 *fou* drunk
10 *clad* dressed up
11 *them they* L (they them SM)

---

[3] *The London Stage*, Pt. 4, 1972–3.

And we's a' git geer enough, we're but young.
    And we're gaily yet, &c.

      Then up wi't Ailie, Ailie, up wi't Ailie, now;   15
      Then up wi't Ailie, quo' cummer, we's get roaring fou.

And one was kissed in the barn,
    Another was kissed on the green,
And t'other behind the pease-stack
    Till the mow flew up to her eyen.   20
      Then up wi't Ailie, Ailie, &c.

Now fie, John Thompson, run,
    Gin ever you ran in your life;
De'il get ye, but hie, my dear Jack,
    There's a mon got to bed with your wife.   25
      Then up wi't Ailie, &c.

Then away John Thompson ran,
    And egad, he ran with speed,
But before he had run his length,
    The false loon had done the deed.   30
      Then up wi't Ailie, &c.

13 *a' git geer* L (a' get geer SM) have got apparel (?)
14 Not in SM
15 *wi't* SM (went L) with it
16 *quo' cummer* SM (quo' Crumma L) said the girl
16 *get* SM (got a L)
19 *And t'other* L (The third SM)
20 *mow* heap of peas
22 *run* L (rin SM)
23 *you ran* SM (ye run L)
24 *ye* L (you SM)
24 *hie* ed. (*hye* L, hey SM) hurry
25 *mon* L (man SM)
25 *to bed* L (a-bed SM)
28 *egad* L (I trow SM)
31 *Then up wi't* (went) *Ailie* L (We're gaily yet SM)